For Sozanno—

Rising in Love

We only rise in love!

Alan Cohen

BY ALAN COHEN

Books:

Are You As Happy As Your Dog?
Companions of the Heart
Dare to Be Yourself
*A Deep Breath of Life
The Dragon Doesn't Live Here Anymore
Have You Hugged Your Monster Today?
I Had It All the Time
*Joy Is My Compass
*Lifestyles of the Rich in Spirit
The Peace That You Seek
*Rising in Love
Setting the Seen

Audiocassettes:

Deep Relaxation
Eden Morning
I Believe in You
Journey to the Center of the Heart (also available as a CD)
Peace

Videocassette:

Dare to Be Yourself

(All of the above are available through Alan Cohen Publications:
800-462-3013. Items marked with an asterisk may also be ordered
by calling Hay House at 800-654-5126.)

Rising in Love

Opening Your Heart in All Your Relationships

Alan Cohen

Hay House, Inc.
Carlsbad, CA

Published and distributed in the United States by: Hay House, Inc.,
P.O. Box 5100, Carlsbad, CA 92018-5100
(800) 654-5126

This book was originally published under the title: *RISING IN
LOVE: The Journey Into Relationship,* Alan Cohen Publications.

Library of Congress Cataloging-in-Publication Data

Cohen, Alan, 1950-
    Rising in love : opening your heart in all your relationships /
Alan Cohen.
        p.   cm.
    ISBN 1-56170-340-0
    1. Spiritual life.   2. Love—Religious aspects.   I. Title.
BL624.C595   1996
158'.2—dc20   96-24369
                                     CIP

ISBN 1-56170-340-0

00 99 98 97 96   6 5 4 3 2
First Printing, 1983, by Alan Cohen Publications
First Printing, Revised Edition, September 1996, Hay House, Inc.
Second Printing, October 1996
Printed in the United States of America

Everyone looks for their calling in love
But I always find it surprising
The way people say that they're falling in love,
When I always felt I was rising

Floating right off of the ground
And reaching something that I only have dreamed of
I'm not falling at all,
I am rising in love

Everyone talks about tying the knot
But I have a hard time agreeing
With the way that we bind up the love that we've got
When the feeling of love should be freeing

Lifting each other up
Instead of giving one another a shove
We won't be falling at all
We'll be rising in love

How do you let love grow?
You've got to give it a chance when you've found it
A bird in your hand will stay
Until you start to close your fingers around it

Love is the river whose waters we test
And a measure of where we are going
But you never can step in the same river twice
For the water is contantly flowing

But the deeper the river, the greater the trust
And the more that we're rising above
We won't be falling at all,
We'll be rising in love

Rising In Love
–David Roth

Author's Introduction

There comes a moment in every person's life when he or she must choose a direction. It is as if there is a fork in the road, and the person standing at the juncture realizes that it is no longer possible to straddle two paths: the time has come to follow one, and follow it wholeheartedly. This sometimes comes as a difficult decision, for it often means that one must release an old and comfortable way of living to venture out into uncharted territory. No one ever said that risk was easy, but all who have taken it exclaim that it is infinitely more rewarding than the familiar. A life is too precious to allow the past to dictate the future. As one visionary proclaimed, *"Life is a daring adventure — or nothing."*

Such a moment of truth came for me when I felt a book seeking to be written, like the gentle but compelling refrain of a celestial song asking to be sung. Because I know so well that every thought we think expands and recreates itself according to its nature, I had to decide what I wanted to plant in this great garden universe. I sensed that I was no longer thinking or living only for myself, but in a way that the entire family of humankind would be affected, changed, and potentially healed. Then I realized that I had before me the opportunity of a lifetime: I had to choose what I would stand for.

I asked myself, "If I could give a gift to humanity, one which would benefit all people and the whole planet and would eventually return to me, what would it be? Immediately the answer came, to my great satisfaction and deep delight: *"Love stands where all else falters."*

So here is a book by, of, about, and for Love. It is the saga of the heart's journey from loneliness to celebration, from empty dark caverns to waterfalls of triumphant gratitude. It is a testimony to the dauntless power of Love to heal broken dreams and make each one of us new, bright, and whole again. It is a book about me, you, and all of us. It is a herald of the happy awakening that no matter what diverse paths our individual destinies take, Love is the Home where we meet and celebrate our reunion as shining rays of one great living Spirit.

As I completed work on the book, I realized that I was given a grace through its writing: I had grown in the process. I had spent months exploring the wonders of Love, only to find Love's wonders living in me. Then it became clear to me that *Rising In Love* is not really my gift to the world, but Love's gift to me. I learned that no one gives without receiving more in return, and now it is my privilege to share what I have received with you.

May the Divine Light in these words serve as a blessing to you and all who read them, and may Love live in your heart as you would know it in your deepest aspiration.

Alan Cohen

The Servants of the Light

There is a scene in that marvelous movie, *Lost Horizon,* in which a group of travelers stranded in the Himalayas is miraculously met by a guide who gives them warm clothing and leads them on a journey that he describes as "not particularly far, but quite difficult." As the voyagers were trekking up the steep, icy footpaths, I noticed that they were all linked together by a long, well-knotted rope, so that if one of them began to slip into the abyss, the combined strength of the fellow travelers would save the one who had slipped.

As I have journeyed through the evolution of *Rising in Love,* I received the grace of many helping hands, friends who contributed loving, positive energy to this book, which has really been a group effort. When we unite for a noble purpose, miracles happen, and that is the story of *Rising in Love.*

I would like to acknowledge some of the fellow travelers with whom I have joined in the ascent. I am deeply grateful to Valerie Johnson for her dedicated and meticulous editing and typesetting, and to Maurice B. Cooke, David Crismond, Jane Visbal, Judy Marlow, Wendy Dompieri, Barbara Cole-Kiernan, and Jeff and Barbara Woolley-Baum for their thoughtful editorial suggestions.

Many thanks to the fine staff at Hay House for their big hearts, high service, and willingness to live the principles they print.

The lyrics in *Rising in Love* sprang from the touching minstrel wisdom of David Roth, who was inspired by the first edition of the book, and who included the song on his album.

It is my grace to be associated with all of the servants of the light. Together we are making it to the top of the mountain.

CONTENTS

The Awakening

Who We Are

Growing Into Greatness

Living in Light

Coming Home

To the teachers of love
who have had the courage
to grow through relationship

The Awakening

Rising In Love

Love is all I ever hope to find here.
        — Seasons of the Heart, John Denver

The first time I fell — rose — in love was when I was seventeen years old. She had red hair, we worked in the same summer camp, and she just happened to have the same last name as me. It was the kind of summer that we all can remember, a season of riding to the beach in open convertibles, walking barefoot over freshly mowed grass, and savoring the sparkling fragrance of the new morning after a long night's rain. It was the kind of summer that lives as a precious jewel in the heart, even through winter storms, for with such a time of year and life came the rediscovery of the shining light of love.

Then I went off to college, and though we were only thirty miles apart, it seemed like ten thousand. I called her nearly every night (for lovers, as you know, time and things exist only to serve love) and she wrote me three letters a day telling me in a thousand different ways how much she loved me. Her specialness was etched into my cells in a magical way that no other person could capture. It sounds pretty schmaltzy now, and it was, but that's how love wins a soul. I was freshly alive and completely complete and every day was a miraculous invitation to find new ways to celebrate the delight of our being together. On our fourth anniversary (four months, that is) I sent a surprise telegram to her in school, and she bolted out of fifth period geometry class, laughing in the face of detention, to call me and tell me that she would love me forever.

Well, for six months at least. By the end of December something had changed. I phoned her one evening to find that she was going to a Hannukah party, and I felt devastated. The thought of her doing something without me was too much for me to bear. (As you can see, the relationship was not exactly founded on the most enlightened unconditional love.) I interpreted her going out as a sign that she no longer

3

loved me (even though she really did), and my immature understanding transformed the energy of love into fear — and there is no more destructive force in the universe than love turned to pain. I blamed her for my hurt, we bickered, and by New Year's Eve it was over. The love that had saved me had deserted me. I had fallen from the giddy peaks of joy into a dark and desolate valley. I had fallen out of love.

As I look back upon the whole experience now, I am extremely grateful, for now I realize I was given a blessing and a lesson. The blessing was that I tasted the nectar of being in love, of cherishing and caring for another human being in a way that her happiness was as important to me as my own, a feeling that somehow made up for all the loneliness that came before it. For a brief moment I was allowed to experience the deepest — and only — purpose of living, which, as far as I know now, is love.

The lesson was that I was not able to sustain that experience because my love had strings on it, strings tied to sandbags of attachments and conditions of what she was supposed to do to prove that she loved me, of what love was supposed to do to prove that it was real. And these are the only chains that keep any of us from rising and living in love always.

In six short months I was shown the great promise of life and the work I needed to do to claim it. Through rising in love and falling out of it, the flower of that relationship left seeds imbued with the wondrous possibility that one day I would again be able to know that precious feeling — but not before I had uprooted the weeds that stood between my experience of Divine Love and its source of light. God showed me a new Sun in the distance, a dazzling light more radiant and fulfilling than any I had ever seen, yet in front of that light loomed the shadows of the mountains that I would have to traverse to come home to it. And that was the way it had to be.

The Promise Fulfilled

*God has the impertinence to not consult the authorities
when he wants to bless someone.*
— Murshid Samuel Lewis, "Sufi Sam"

Fourteen years, countless slings and arrows of outrageous fortune,
nearly unbelievable miracles of Grace, and a number of fallen gurus
later, I found myself sitting in the parking lot of Grand Union one spring
afternoon. The string of events that led me there was woven by a Divine
design far more imaginative than I can begin to explain; it seems that
God has His own ideas about where and when and how He wants to
appear, and I think He gets a certain kind of cosmic kick out of surprising us.

It was in just such a seemingly unlikely place that I rose in love
once again. This time not with a redhead, but with the cheerful little
fellow who collects the shopping baskets. I was just sitting in my car
minding my own business when he wheeled by, and all of a sudden
an overwhelming feeling of love welled up within me, as if I was
beholding the most beautiful person on earth. Yes, he was wearing combat boots, his hair was a little greasy, and his posture wasn't the greatest,
but he was God. He was just so radiant, so full of light, that all I wanted
to do was sit and look at him shuffle those carts to the rhythm of his
happy whistling.

Then, just as his tune had become mine, I was cut off by a very
ordinary-looking women in a very ordinary-looking car making a
beeline for a parking space. And because love lifts the mundane into
the miraculous, I was so pleased to see her go before me. As she glided
into that space our eyes met and immediately I rose in love with her,
too. I was enraptured with the perfection of her plainness. Ensouled
in that delightfully honest being was the Light of God, and I decided
that He had cloaked her in such a simple form to underline the glory
of utter Innocence. Her inner beauty outshined all the designs of men,

5

and I knew that we were brought together for the sheer wonder of celebrating the presence of goodness in every breath of creation.

As my beloved stepped out of her car and into the supermarket, my attention was captured by a loud "Woof!" from the Country Squire station wagon next to me. There, with his stately snout perched on the open back window, was the most effervescent German Shepherd with whom I have ever connected, twinkling right at me. Immediately I realized that he was a high soul who took a canine incarnation to woof the Divine Love Song. And in that moment all I wanted to do was dash into Grand Union and buy him every Milkbone I could find. That's just the way it is when you're in love. That's just the way it is.

Believe in Yourself

Believe in yourself as God believes in you.
— The Wiz

A few nights ago I was feeling a little down, a little empty, a little like I'm not making it. Then, as I was going to sleep I began to think of the people in my life who have believed in me, who have found worth or goodness in me even — and especially — when I wasn't believing in myself. These were the special friends, like guardian angels who were there for me when I needed them most. I cherish acts of loving kindness, for they were precious gifts of confidence that helped sustain me through times like the other night. If I may, I would like to share some of them with you now.

In the fifth grade I developed a tremendous crush on Marie Keller, a ten-year-old strawberry blonde girl with freckles and glasses, who lived in Camp Kilmer because her father was in the army. She didn't know it, but I was wild about her. I used to think about her all the time. Every day I would look up her number in the telephone book (even though I never got up the nerve to call her), and the highlight of my school year was when I picked her up (lifted her up, that is) in the cloak room so she could get her yellow rainhat off the rack, which was too high for her to reach.

Round about the end of that year I learned that her father was being transferred to France, which meant that she would be moving and I would probably never see her again. So I wrote her a long love letter on that thin yellow paper with green lines, you know the kind they give you in the fifth grade to learn how to write. I wrote that I thought she was the nicest girl I had ever met, and I really liked her a lot, and I was sorry she was moving. I signed it *A Secret Admirer*, probably because I felt so crummy about myself that I thought that if she ever found out it was me, she would tell me that she didn't like

7

me, and I would feel devastated. So it was safer and easier to love her from afar and not have to face the possibility of rejection. I sent her the letter and left the rest up to fate.

I heard no news or response. Could the letter have gotten lost? Did the army intercept it and turn it over to the CIA for investigation? Could it have been sent to the *Dead Letter File*? I almost wished I had signed it.

Then, on the last day of school, my teacher, Mrs. Montague, the first teacher I ever trusted, took me out in the hall and asked, "Alan, are you going to say good-bye to Marie?"

"What do you mean?" I played it cool.

"Well, I know how much you like her."

"What do you mean, 'I like her'?" I played it cooler.

But because it's hard to conceal a crush in the fifth grade, and because my ability to act phony was not yet well-developed, Mrs. Montague knew.

"Alan, I know you wrote that letter to Marie."

That did it. I burst out in hysterical tears. I don't really know why. Maybe I was embarrassed. Maybe the pain of hiding was too great. Maybe my fears were brought to their knees by the power of Mrs. Montague's tender compassion. Whatever it was, I cried and cried — bawled is more like it — more than I can remember crying in my whole life.

Mrs. Montague put her arm around me and told me with a softness in her voice that I shall never forget, "Alan, there's no reason to cry . . . Do you know what Marie told me when she got that letter? . . . She said it was the nicest thing anyone has ever done for her, and it made her the happiest girl in the world!"

Well, I don't really remember what happened after that. All I remember is the tenderness that Mrs. Montague showed me in the hall as the other kids walked by, asking, "What's he crying about?" Mrs. Montague was there for me. She believed in me enough to take me seriously. She understood me in just the way I needed to be loved at that moment. Thank you, Mrs. Montague. May your kindness be returned to you a hundredfold.

As I consider this story and the others I am about to relate, I see that they pretty much were the times when I felt or acted like a real boob, when I wasn't exactly the most sophisticated or debonair person. And it occurs to me as well that these were the times when I most needed someone to believe in me, when my own ability to love myself was at a low ebb, and when God compassionately gave me that missing love through the arms of another.

During that same year the most important thing that a human being could do (as I perceived the universe) was to play baseball. The world, as far as I was concerned, was divided into two very distinct camps: The New York Yankees and their fans (*Us*), and everyone else (*Them* — The Wrong Side). In my world, Mickey Mantle was the High Guru, to get a box seat behind third base at Yankee Stadium was like receiving an audience with the Dalai Lama, and my loftiest dreams featured me making a daring catch of a long fly ball up against the 417-foot centerfield fence in the House That Ruth Built. I lived for baseball.

That summer I played first base on the championship Little League team, the St. Sebastian Giants. (There's another miracle for you; I was the only Cohen on a team of thirty skinny, olive-complexioned kids, all of whose names ended in "ini," "isi," or "io," and whose fathers all happened to coincidently be members of the St. Sebastian Lodge that sponsored the team. Someone in a very high place (maybe even St. Sebastian himself) had to pull some strings to get me on that team.

The season came down to the final game of the playoffs. It was the bottom of the last inning, score tied, runner on third — a situation worthy of Howard Cosell's most delicious fantasies. The pitch . . . Batter connects . . . Ground ball to Cohen at first! . . . The runner breaks for the plate! . . . The catcher braces for the throw . . . Runner slides . . . The throw! . . . A billowing cloud of dirt explodes around the plate as all the parents rise from their multi-colored lawn chairs, eagerly stretching their necks to catch a glimpse of the final verdict. The park reverberates with the bark of the umpire, forever confirming the Champions of the League!

To make a long, sad story short and to spare me the agony of great embarrassment, I'll just say that Cohen at first made a throw very well put for a ten-foot-tall catcher, but which no eleven-year-old kid on this planet would ever have a prayer of catching. The game was over. The season was over. We lost. I had made the losing throw. Pretty heavy karma. I felt lower than Judas. I burst out crying (it was a very good year for my tear ducts), and as the other team was whooping and hollering and jumping on each others' shoulders, the two coaches of my team

headed right for me. I just knew that I was about to receive the worst
chewing out of my life.

But it never came. Instead, Coach Santisi put his arm around my
shoulder and said, "That's O.K., Alan . . . It's just a game . . . We'll
get 'em next year!"

Well, next year never came — we didn't make it to the playoffs.
But, you see, it didn't really matter. What mattered was that Coach
Santisi was willing to forgive me, willing to encourage me when I was
condemning myself. And that made me a winner.

Many years passed, and one summer morning in 1972 I found
myself driving up a California mountain with my friend Jim, a very
unusual guy — also a very holy and Godly guy. It was only appropriate
that we were driving a redecorated '62 VW bus with psychedelic
cushions in the back and a silver sticker on the hood that proclaimed
"*U.S.A. in Space!*" That about summed us up.

It was also appropriate that a State Trooper should pull us over
for driving too slow in the fast lane. (We had renounced time.) Unfortunately, the trooper was still in time and he decided that time was
still important enough to write me a ticket for not respecting it. This
time I did not burst out crying, but I was a little distraught.

As the policeman began to write the ticket, I saw Jim get out of
our van and approach the police car.

"Get back in your vehicle!" yelled the trooper from behind his door,
as if we were aliens from another planet, come to invade California
and hijack it to another galaxy. It made me wonder if he was more
afraid of us than we were of him. (And if he was, I wouldn't blame him.)

So Jim approached him more slowly, with open hands to show
he had no ray-gun. Then, to my utter amazement I saw Jim put his
arm around the trooper's shoulder and begin to walk him back to our
bus. As they approached I heard these words from Jim:

"You know, this guy you're giving the ticket to does some very
important work!"

"Oh?"

"Yes, he certainly does! . . . He is a 'Human Relations Trainer!'
Do you know what that is?"

"No, what's that?"

Sitting at the wheel of the van, right next to our copy of *Be Here
Now*, I had to do all I could to keep from laughing. First of all, I couldn't

believe that there was something that a native Californian hadn't heard of, but more significantly I couldn't believe what Jim was telling this guy. Was he putting him on? Was he serious? Was he just trying to get out of a ticket? Whatever it was, it was priceless.

"That man at the wheel teaches people how to communicate, and I'm sure that you, in your line of work, know how important communication is . . . I imagine they taught you all about communication at the Academy, didn't they?"

"Well, I think they did have something about that."

By this time I was sitting back, enjoying every frame of this scene, like a Marx Brothers-Woody Allen-Ingmar Bergman movie with a thousand possible endings, none of which I could imagine, but all of which I knew would be simultaneously cosmic and ridiculous.

"Oh, I'm sure they did include that in your work," Jim went on. "Communication is so important these days. It makes all the difference between harmony and tension in our world. I'm convinced that if we could all just communicate more with each other, this world would be a much safer and happier place to live in!"

"Yes, I think you're right," agreed the officer as he handed me the ticket.

But at that point it really didn't matter whether or not I got the ticket. The situation had been miraculously transformed from what it had started out to be; it had grown from two hippies encountering a State Trooper to three souls meeting on a mountain. Jim was not putting the officer on and he was not just trying to get out of the ticket. He was serious.

You see, Jim saw that meeting as an opportunity to reach out and make contact with another human being. His love of life and his appreciation for the richness of humanity was so great that he could not be intimidated by belief systems about getting a traffic ticket. As far as Jim could see, three souls were being connected in a novel way, and here was a chance to celebrate. Jim used every moment to lift the worldly into the Light. He is one of the few people I know who can turn a traffic ticket into a gift, a potential arrest into service, and a sticky situation into mutual upliftment.

The faith Jim held in the Divinity of that encounter, like the confidence my teacher and coach held in me, have served me as shining examples of how we can support each other along road to enlightenment.

RISING IN LOVE

Let's return for a moment to that Himalayan footpath in *Lost Horizon*, upon which those courageous voyagers steadily tread. As they were struggling over the crags and precipices, tied together by that rope which kept them from falling, it occurred to me that they were united by an even more crucial, more powerful bond: *the common belief that they could make it*, and that they could make it *together*. They had to believe in themselves enough to keep going while the winds howled in their faces and their muscles ached to no end. They had to have a vision of success that far transcended and outshined their personal frailties. Each one had to trust that the others would not let him down, and — more importantly — they had to trust themselves not to let the others down. They had to believe in themselves.

After braving the cold, steep climb, the voyagers finally made it over the crest of the mountain. There they found themselves in a completely different, amazing place: *Shangri-La* — the land of eternal contentment. They entered a realm of tropical sunshine, sparkling waterfalls, and a community of gentle people living in harmonious cooperation. This peaceful way of life, so unlike the harsh world from which they came, made every hard step to reach it worthwhile. Their finding it was the reward of their willingness to persevere.

Though we may not climb the Himalayas, each of us must traverse the mountains of our own self. This is the only real journey there is — and the most difficult. Yet we can — and will — succeed as we realize that we can make it, if we just *believe that we can*. There really *is* a *Shangri-La*, and an Emerald City of Oz, and a Kingdom of Heaven; it does not matter what we call it, for they are all one. What matters is that we know it is there — indeed it is already *here* — waiting for us to discover it within our very hearts, at the end of the path that begins with the first step of believing in our self.

Who We Are

Original Innocence

We are stardust. We are golden.
— Joni Mitchell

There is a scene in *The Empire Strikes Back* which pretty well sums up who we are and what we need to do to remember it. Luke Skywalker, after undergoing intensive training as a Jedi master, finds himself face-to-face with Darth Vader, the personification of Evil. As the two engage in perilous light-sabre combat, Lord Vader has Luke backed up against a bottomless precipice that drops, it seems, to a black pit at the end of the universe.

Darth Vader cannot, however, afford to kill Skywalker because he realizes the power that Luke has gained as a master of The Force, and Vader wants to use this power for his own evil purposes. (Evil has no power of its own; it is simply God's power turned inside out.)

"Luke!" appeals the dark one, with a clenched fist raised above his head. "Join with me! Together we will rule the universe!"

"I shall not, Darth Vader!" cries Luke as the winds of the bottomless pit howl behind him, "Not after you killed my father, whom I have never seen!"

"Luke," answers Vader in a long sardonic whisper, ". . . I *am* your father!"

Upon hearing these words, Luke Skywalker's eyes open wide in astonishment. The possibility is too terrible to contemplate. But then, because Luke is disciplined as a knight of The Force, he regains his composure. Luke thinks within himself for a moment and then cries, "NOOOOOOOO!" with a certainty that reverberates to the far reaches of the galaxy. With this affirmation Luke lets go his hold on the ledge and allows himself to fall down, down, down through a myriad of portals and passageways and finally out the bottom of this planet that Darth Vader has conquered. Luke's training as a master, you see, gave him more trust in the unknown than in the words of the evil one.

15

Then, just at the final portal of the planet, Luke is able to grab onto one last ledge where he hangs by one hand, literally at the edge of creation. At this crucial moment Princess Leia, having just escaped from the city-planet herself, psychically hears Luke's cry for help. Immediately she turns her craft around and scoops Luke up just as he is about to fall.

Every day, perhaps every moment, I am faced with Luke Skywalker's decision, and so are we all. It comes down to who we believe we are, and who we think our Father is. Do we think that we are born of evil, or do we know that our Source is a shining light? Are we willing to compromise our integrity for the sake of worldly power, or do we have the faith to let go and trust that we will be taken care of, even if we don't sign the devil's bargain? Are we really unknown, purposeless creatures that have come into a haphazard world by a sardonic twist of misfortune, or are we godly beings, sprung forth from a magnificent lifestream of Spirit, ever growing and blossoming into greater wonder? Simply, is the Spark of God within us, or is it not?

Frankly, I've had enough of worshipping original sin, and I'm about ready for some Original Innocence. I've been in the presence of a good number of little babies lately, and there is nothing at all sinful about them. They are made only of light with a holy little body to shine it into the world. I recently had the blessing to see a radiant little girl, Vanessa Rose, when she was just three hours old, and the energy around her was so pure, so chaste, so Divine. When I put my face near hers I felt the brightness of a bouquet of dew-laden wild flowers, newly sprung on an early May morning. She was vibrating in such a clear light that I just wanted to trade in every thought that I have ever had about good and evil and just hold this little angelic being in my arms. I found no original sin in that child.

If there is any such thing as original sin, it is a learned experience. We take on a self-image of sinfulness when we believe that we are no good, that there is something we must do to prove our worthiness, that we must earn love because we are bad. I recently met a young man who turned down an excellent job offer with a major corporation because he was afraid he might fail if he accepted the position. I asked him if he had ever done an age regression to see how he learned that fear. He told me that he could not remember past the age of five.

"What happened at age five?" I asked.

16

"One day I dropped one of my father's tools and broke it, and when he found out he locked me in the closet and told me that he would never let me out because I was such a rotten kid."

So that's how original sin got started. We cannot condemn the father, for that is probably pretty much how his father dealt with him. And his father. And his father. And so on. Original sin is nothing more than a wrong idea that got started somewhere way back by someone who didn't remember original innocence. That's all it is.*

Original innocence is what Luke Skywalker had to remember to say "No!" to Darth Vader's assertion that he was Luke's father. Luke had to make a very clear choice about who he was. Years ago I was given a teaching that has helped me to make this choice, words that have stayed with me in a very deep way:

WE ARE SPIRITUAL BEINGS
GOING THROUGH A MATERIAL EXPERIENCE

This was the precious awareness that enabled Luke to rise above evil attempting to seduce him into believing he was born of darkness, and not light. It was the ancient memory that gave him the strength to turn his back on a life that was not true to his heart's aspiration. And it is the very awareness that you and I need to remember — and practice — a thousand times a day, whenever we are assailed with questions, fears, or doubts about our self-worth or dignity. It is the affirmation that carries us past television commercials that tell us we need to brush with *Ultrabrite* to have sex appeal, or when we see newspaper headlines purposely fabricated to arouse emotions of fear or indignation, or when we watch an irate taxi driver shake his fist at us for driving at a

---

*There actually is a basis for the idea of original sin, but it is an esoteric principle far more positive and reasonable than the idea of guilt, shame, fear, and unworthiness that many people believe it to be. Original sin has been misunderstood because it has often been taught by persons who have unconsciously projected their own unresolved guilt and fear to students.

Original sin is the limitation of awareness that a human being experiences when he or she comes into — takes the consciousness of — a human body. To enter the earth plane in a physical body, we narrow the range of our awareness to concentrate our attention on a particular karma that needs to be worked out. This is similar to a general of an army leaving his view of the battlefield from the top of a plateau to go into the valley to confer with a particular lieutenant needing special guidance and instructions. For a temporary period the high perspective of the whole scene is lost, but it is a purposeful act for the sake of focusing attention on one area that will eventually contribute

reasonable speed. It is the truth that we must hold on to when it seems that the world has gone crazy and there is no God. We must constantly say "No!" to all that would offer to make us whole, for such a "No!" is a resounding "Yes!" to the truth that we are *already* whole, and could never be otherwise.

Why, then, have we not lived in constant abiding awareness of our wholeness? We simply had a case of spiritual absent-mindedness, Cosmic Amnesia. We used to know, we started out knowing, but somewhere along the way we forgot; we became distracted into thinking that we are less than Divine. We believed someone who threatened to keep us locked in a closet because he forgot the goodness of his own self. And the glorious conclusion of this whole melodrama is that even though we seemed to forget how to love ourselves, we still remain Skywalkers. Our forgetting, you see, could never change our identity. Our attack thoughts could never touch our invulnerability. Our heritage is eternally ensured. The outcome of the story is a happy one.

The day after I saw *The Empire Strikes Back*, I went out to jog. After a while I began to feel tired and I wanted to quit. A little mind-voice began to say, "You really should stop . . . You're getting tired . . . You may hurt yourself . . . Go home." But as I heard the way this voice was speaking to me, I recognized it to be the voice of Darth Vader telling me I am his son, for his voice is the voice of limitation, unworthiness, and fear. So I decided that every time I heard the voice of "You can't do anymore!" I would answer, "Oh, yes I can! I am *not* the son of Darth Vader! I am free, not subservient to small thoughts! I belong to the Light, and the Light is of God!" I had to mentally keep yelling these affirmations, constantly, vehemently fighting against the

---

to the success of the forces as a whole.

When we took birth we purposely entered a world founded on the erroneous premise of separateness, so we could rectify that unconsciousness by becoming aware that there is only unity. We played the game of name, form, and difference because there was a mistaken belief that those ideas were real, and we had to enter their domain to discover and know the God within them. Symbolically, we had to go into the basement and get our feet wet to fix the leak.

Seen in this light, original sin is not a matter of being bad, wrong, or evil. It is a positive evolutionary step the soul takes to grow into greater light. Further, the soul is offering a great act of sacrifice to leave its universal awareness and take on a temporary unconsciousness. For this reason we all owe great thanks to every human being who ever lived—including ourselves—for we chose to come to earth to serve God simply by being here.

assertions of limitation. Finally the voice disintegrated (behind his in-
timidating mask, Darth Vader has no face), and I just kept running
. . . and running . . . and running. For miles. The voice that told me
I couldn't go on was a liar.

We can all go on for miles. It does not have to be jogging. In fact,
it does not really matter what we do, as long as we push on long enough
to laugh at an empty black mask. It can be handling a difficult family,
or learning to harmonize with a demanding boss, or forgiving. I am
becoming convinced that we can all do anything we set our mind on.
We just have to remember who we are, and that we can. Sometimes
it is not easy. Sometimes we may find ourselves face-to-face with the
Lord of the Dark Empire, and sometimes we may find ourselves, like
Luke Skywalker, hanging on for dear life at the end of a slender thread
over what seems to be a bottomless abyss. But as long as we remember
that we are Skywalkers we shall find ourselves safe in the arms of an
unvanquishable Force of Love that somehow heard our stand for Truth
and had no alternative but to come to our rescue on a starship of Light
with its course set on Home.

Angels in a Strange Land

Toto, I've a feeling we're not in Kansas anymore!
                                                    — Dorothy

"He was a student of Confucius in a past life," Hilda explained as she began the class, "and then he was a revered sage on his own merit."

"Wow! This is fascinating!" I thought, as my ears perked up.

"I usually don't delve into people's past lives," she went on, "but in his case it was necessary to help him understand what he has gone through in this life." I wanted to hear more.

"You can see why it was so hard for Bill to adjust to the lifestyle in modern America. He had developed very deep intuitions and talents in previous lives, and when he took birth in an average family in the Midwest, his parents did not understand the sensitivity of his soul. As a child he would stay by himself and be fascinated with his art work, an aptitude he had carried over from previous lives. When his mother would yell, 'Stop with your games, Billy, and hurry down to the kitchen — it's time for dinner!' you can understand what a jarring experience it was for him."

Hilda went on to explain that many people, like Billy, have had difficulty adjusting to this life because their souls are used to more subtle and spiritual environments, and the harsh vibrations of the contemporary world are very rough for them. This story was an eye-opening lesson for me: If you or I didn't fit in with the normal crowd, it may not have been because there was something wrong with us; perhaps our souls were a little disoriented by the culture into which we were born, and we required a number of years to find our niche.

One of my favorite scenes in the movie *Godspell* is that of the calling of the disciples. The story begins with John the Baptist staunchly striding over the Brooklyn Bridge, blowing the conch to announce the coming of the light. Then, throughout the city we see men and women in many different occupations stopping what they are doing to hearken

21

to the call: a ballerina leaps from the shoulders of her hero and dances out the door; a taxi driver at a jammed intersection quits tooting his horn and leaves his cab right there with the door open; a school teacher walks out of his classroom to find the Real Teacher; and so on. Each one responds to a powerful prompting and all of them converge at the Central Park fountain to meet Jesus, John, and their baptism with destiny.

So it is with the gathering of the community of the spirit, now quickening ever more rapidly as the foundation of a new world manifests before our eyes. There really is a New Age coming, a new way of living in spiritual light on earth, and you who somehow feel drawn to read this, and I who feel guided to write it, have *chosen* to come to this stormy planet at this critically significant time for the specific purpose of awakening ourselves and our world to the return of harmony on earth. Our feelings that there *must* be more to life than struggling to earn a living and becoming vice president of the company and having a house in the suburbs, were born of an aspiration that burned more deeply in our hearts than those suggested to us as children. And it is by the same mysteriously exciting plan that we have somehow become connected with one another as links of light in a group commitment to work for the restoration of love on the planet earth.

We live in a strange time, a time when we have been taught that we must apologize for believing in God. We live in a time when women, homosexuals, and blacks have successfully emerged into the richness of self-appreciation, but the lovers of God have wandered down the alleyways of psychic sensationalism and fallen prey to unscrupulous cult leaders because there just haven't been enough pure teachers of Truth to gather the Children of Light into their arms. It is a time represented by a woman in one of my classes at a major industry, who whispered to me that the class techniques are similar to the ones that inspire her at her prayer meetings, but she couldn't say "God" out loud at work, for that sort of thing just isn't talked about there. It is a time that is begging us to bravely and honestly ask, *"Who am I?"* and then see if we are living the highest truth we know.

It is a time when many persons are experiencing spiritual awakening, but who have not had people around them to give them encouragement or support to nurture these gifts. When I used to go into a high school health class to lecture, I would ask if anyone had ever had any spiritual or psychic experiences. Hardly any hands would go up. Then, as soon as the class was over and most of the class had filed out the door, there would always be three or four students who would come up to me and tell me, "You know, sometimes I lie in bed at night and close my eyes and I see the most beautiful colors," or "I saw an angel when I was little, but my mother told me I was imagining it," or "I had a dream that my grandma was going to die, and then she did, and I felt guilty because I thought I caused it." And then nearly all of them would tell me, ". . . but I have never told anyone about this because I am afraid people would think I'm weird."

One of these students, a tenth-grader who sat by himself on the bus because nobody would talk to him, came to one of my evening yoga classes. After the class he asked me a question about meditation that I didn't even understand until I had been meditating for a few more years. No wonder he sat by himself on the bus.

There are many persons of like nature in mental institutions, not because they are insane, but because they are very sensitive souls who have not been able to bring their social act into harmony with the lunacy that the rest of us call "normal." I have several keenly introspective friends who have been in and out of community mental health centers because the people around them were not sufficiently spiritually aware to understand what these people were about, and they convinced the "problem" people that they were "not well," while they were simply travelling to the beat of a different drummer. A good deal of mental patients do not lack mental health, but are unskilled actors in relation to the masses who have learned to suffocate their real sanity under lives that revolve around a mass pact of mutual foolishness.

As I write these words the faces and names of my "mentally ill" friends are coming to my mind, and my heart goes out to them (and really to all of us) for these are some of the most beautiful, sensitive, and loving souls that I have known in this life, souls who have so much spiritual insight that they could heal the insanity of this world with their purity, if only they had the courage to believe in themselves. I have read their poetry, listened to their songs, and been privy to their journals, and many of their works are not unlike those of Da Vinci, Brahms, and Blake. The difference is that the acknowledged masters are allowed the license of oddity because they are acclaimed as geniuses, while the modern schizophrenics have not had enough supportive persons around them who could see beyond idiosyncracy and into the light.

And because there really is no injustice, these mental patients are where they are because they have lessons to learn. Not lessons of mental health, for many of them are healthier than some of the doctors who treat them. Their lessons are ones of *discrimination* and *communication*. They need to learn who they can tell about the voices they hear. The trick is to know who to tell, how, and where. It's very interesting to me who we accept as a genuine prophet. Moses heard a voice speak to him from a burning bush, saying, *"I Am that I Am,"* and the entire nation of Israel followed him to freedom through the parted waters of the Red Sea. My friend Arthur Marmelstein heard the same voice and now he is locked up in Bellevue.

I wonder how well Moses or Jesus would be received if they brought their same message today. I have a feeling it would depend on how well they delivered it. Jesus knew how to play the game. Yes, he was eventually outcast, but only after he had finished his chosen mission and he was ready to fulfill his destiny of going on the cross. It is important to recognize that he kept it very well together for the three years that he needed to complete his ministry. He was the master *par excellence* of human relations and interpersonal communication. That is why he said, "A prophet is never accepted in his home town," "Cast not pearls before swine,"* and "If someone does not accept your teaching, shake the dust off your feet and move on."

The downfall of many of those who realize their Godhood is that they tell the wrong people in the wrong way too soon. Someone has a genuine spiritual insight and runs to his dad or his professor or his shrink and tells them, "I am the Christ" — a career about which most Jewish fathers are not too thrilled. The second mistake they (we) make is that when they tell everyone, "I am God," or "I am the Christ," they forget to throw in "and so are you." Godhood, you see, is a very delicate issue to discuss in mixed company. It's a little like playing army. Everyone wants to be the General and no one wants to be in the infantry. So people get a little threatened when you say, "God is in me," because, quite naturally, they want God to be in them, too. If He is in you and not me, that is a little scary to the ego. So all you have

---

*So as not to demean any of God's children, let it be clear that Jesus was not referring to *people* as swine, but to the foolish thoughts of limitation that people believed, unbridled beasts that would tear delicate truths to shreds by analyzing them to death.

to say is, ". . . and He is in you, too," and that will minimize your chances of being incarcerated. The bottom line is that everybody wants to be acknowledged as godly, which is really correct, so we might as well do it.

If I think that I'm Jesus Christ, I'm in big trouble, for although the Christ is in everyone, there was only one Jesus. If I fall into this category I had better go back to the spiritual drawing board and scrutinize my source, or else I'm in for some pretty stiff competition. There was a book that I heard about in college, *The Three Christs of Ypsilanti,* about three men in a mental institution in Ypsilanti, Michigan, each of whom believed he was Jesus Christ. A psychologist there had the fascinating idea to put these three fellows in a room together, lock the door, and see what happened. (A very interesting idea, was it not?) The outcome, as I understand, was that one of the fellows succeeded in convincing the other two that he was the *real* Jesus Christ, and they ended up becoming his disciples. Well, it's a cute story, but as far as I can see, they all missed the point. The only way they could all emerge victorious — like all of us — is to realize that Christ lives equally in everyone.

Perhaps, then, it has been wise — and necessary — that the community of the spiritually awakened has stayed in the wings for so long, for to sow the seeds of the New Age in a spiritually parched terrain would have cost the movement its life. But that has changed drastically, now. The urgency of the times, the stakes of nuclear power, the plunder of the mother earth, have all pushed the closet spiritualists out into the open. Now we have no choice but to connect with all the Truth we know and generate as much light as God can pour through us. We are now forced to step into our calling. The rain of worldly confusion has come as blessed nourishment to the seeds of the New Age, planted like tulip bulbs last fall, dormant during the winter of ruthless winds, and now sprouting with the gentle spring rain. Of course God's timing is perfect.

So that is where we stand. The marriage of necessity and courage has lifted God's people above the old taskmaster of fear of popular opinion, brought renaissance to the strength of the mystic saints, and turned over the clodded ground to breathe new life into fertile seedbeds. And the light from this new willingness to make a stand for Truth is very bright indeed. I recently discovered a wonderful essay in *The*

Washington Monthly (February, 1982), entitled *"God is My Chiropractor: Confessions of a Closet New Ager,"* publicizing the testimony of Art Levine:

> *I've decided to come out of the closet. For nearly two years I have been engaging in illicit practices that have scandalized my friends and set me apart from the mainstream of American intellectual life. Possessed by strong drives that I have been helpless to control, I've become part of a hidden subculture . . . Like millions of others with similar preferences, I have attempted, with some success, to pass as part of the conventional world . . . But all the while, I have been concealing my strange secret life.*
>
> *Over the last few years . . . growing numbers of us have surfaced and proclaimed our unusual predilections . . . Naturally we've all been branded kooks and weirdos . . .*
>
> *Now it is my turn to reveal myself, and, I hope, make it easier for those who feel the same forbidden stirrings within themselves. The truth must be told:*
>
> *I BELIEVE IN GOD AND I PRAY EVERY DAY!*

I confess, too, that Art Levine speaks for me, and I believe he captures a bit of all of us. The sad irony of our world is that deep down inside, everyone wants God to be real. Perhaps not everyone would choose the word "God," but it really doesn't matter. Every one of us has a feeling for joy, for spirit, for love, for goodness, for trusting, for caring, for reverence for life. Even *Buick* and *Miller Beer* commercials are founded on humankind's love for "the free spirit in us all" and the High Life. These are the great common denominators of all humankind, the lofty yet reachable ideals that we do not need an anthropological study to prove, the glories of existence that far transcend whatever we call them. They are the spiritual glue that binds us all together.

It is but a great charade, a human masquerade that keeps us from really getting close to — *grokking** — one another. Recently I went

---

*grok: If we made a big soup of all of us and we all drank it, we would all become one.
— Robert Heinlein, *Stranger in a Strange Land.*

to a gathering at the home of a woman who had invited a number of people to form a spiritual support group. I arrived to join the most boring conversation I have ever experienced, purely intellectual, completely empty. The vagueness in that room was enough to put the Superbowl to sleep. I was equally responsible; my words were without conviction. I couldn't wait for the whole thing to be over so I could go home and watch TV or eat, both of which promised more substance than this conversation.

Then one person turned the whole scene around. She said right up front, "I have come to this group because I love God very much, and He is more important to me than anything else in my life. I am here because I am hoping that this group can help bring God more deeply into my life." You would not believe how quickly the energy in that room became alive and empowered. The moment she said that, nearly all the eyes in that room lit up, people sat up straighter and leaned toward the center of the circle, the wiggling and scratching and looking at the clock ceased, and something very important happened in that room. All because one person had the courage to say "*I love God.*" That made it alright for the rest of us, myself included, to say it also. Then the next person said, "You know, that's exactly how I'm feeling, too, but I didn't know if this was the right group to say it in." And the next person. And the next. In a chain reaction the acknowledgement of the presence of God filled the atmosphere and I tell you that living room became a real living room, filled with the Holy Spirit to match any church anywhere. The evening concluded with each of us saying a prayer out loud, and I want to tell you the prayers were among the most powerful I have ever experienced. The light in that room was indescribable. All because one person had the guts to say "*I love God.*"

It takes courage to rise above the status quo, a bravery that each of us must learn in our own way. I am reminded of a week in college when I met a very nice girl at a fraternity party. The next Saturday night we went out to the movies, after which we went back to her dorm room. She sat on one side of the couch and I sat at the other. I really wanted to sit close to her and put my arm around her, but I hesitated to make the first move; I was afraid of being rejected. So there I sat, making believe I was interested in talking about the school football team and religion classes and psychology (this conversation rivaled the one above for the boredom award), until the buzzer sounded and it was

27

time for me to leave. (This was in the unliberated days before coed dorms.) Then, after we had been going out for a few months and I had made it over to the other side of the couch, we talked about that first date.

"You know," she told me, "I really wanted to sit close to you, too, but I was afraid you'd reject me, and I was waiting for you to make the first move!"

So there we had sat, two dunderheads, both wanting very much to get together, talking about nothing, yet feeling very much something, and neither of us doing anything about it.

That, as I see it, is pretty much where spiritual action has been for a long time, at least my spiritual action. We have been sitting on opposite ends of the couch, waiting for the other person to make the first move, waiting for someone else to let us know that it's O.K. to say "God," that it's O.K. to feel beautiful, that it's O.K. to love. But if we all wait for the other guy to do it first, who will do it? That is why the world has been the way it has been; very few of us have had the courage to be the first one in a crowd to say who we are. Lincoln said it. Gandhi made a stand for it. Martin Luther King, Jr. lived it. Now you and I have our moment of opportunity.

We don't have to all write a Gettysburg address or march to the Indian shore or lead a social revolution. And we don't have to all go around saying, "I love God" (although that might be kind of nice). We just have to remember who we are and treat each other like who we are. We need to accept the fact that every one of us is a precious piece of Living Spirit, and that spirit is very much affected by how we treat each other. The big lie of life is that we are tough, immovable, unaffectable islands in space, and the great Truth is that *how we touch one another can really heal our world*, right down to how we say "thank you" for the change at the supermarket. Then the way we ask for a stamp at the post office becomes a prayer meeting; answering the telephone, communion; and our smiles, living placards. This is how we make space for one another to come out of hiding. Every time one person says, "You're beautiful," or "Thank you for you," or "Let's work this out together," that is one more hand extended to bring one more misunderstood mental patient out of feeling lost and into creativity. That is one more sensitive young artist who doesn't have to put aside his crayons just because it's time for dinner. And that is one less lonely high school boy who has to sit by himself on the bus because his schoolmates just wouldn't understand.

Heroes-At-Large

I am a promise. I am a possibility.
I am a great big bundle of potentiality.

— Children's song

I was introduced to a retarded fellow named Mickey. The friend who introduced us told me that Mickey was classified as an "idiot-savant," someone who is half retarded and half a genius. As we sat together waiting for a bus, my friend asked Mickey, "Say, what day of the week did St. Patrick's Day come on in 1963?" Mickey went through some rapid mental computations and within about five seconds blurted out, "That was a Sunday!" We consulted a calendar, and Mickey was correct. He asked Mickey a few more similar questions, and he was accurate every single time. While Mickey was not sufficiently mentally proficient to cook a meal or drive a car, part of his brain was developed thousands of times superior to most people.

So it is with all of us. Each in our own way we're a little uncoordinated, but we have some tremendous possibilities. The trick is to bring it all together, to let our latent greatness blossom until we're all we can be. Then is our destiny fulfilled.

There was a movie out not long ago, *Hero-At-Large*, about a shy, unsuccessful actor whose confidence in himself is waning with each rejection at the casting office. The only job he can find is that of impersonating the famous Captain Avenger, signing autographs for children outside a theatre where the latest Captain Avenger movie is being shown. We see him at the end of his evening's work as he is being picked up by a chartered bus, taking his seat among forty other Captain Avengers with forty pens in hand, all of them disheartened and disappointed in themselves just as he is.

The plot thickens when on his way home that night he happens upon a grocery store robbery. Without thinking about it, he dashes

29

behind a display, throws off his overcoat and trousers, and emerges in full Captain Avenger uniform (Ta-Daaaa!). Donning the well-known crusader's mask, he bravely confronts the thugs, whose resistance is no match, of course, for Captain Avenger. The crooks flee, dropping the loot behind them, and our hero disappears into the night without revealing his true identity, leaving Mr. and Mrs. Grocery Store Owner beaming with their jaws agape.

Word gets around the city that Captain Avenger is real, safeguarding innocent victims, rescuing the helpless, and valiantly serving the public good. Newspaper and television stories glorify the mysterious man of good conscience, children idolize his bravery, and there is a new era of hopefulness in the heart of the metropolis.

But not in the heart of one bewildered Captain Avenger. The more he hears of Captain Avenger's glory, the deeper our hero becomes plunged in depression, for he knows that Captain Avenger is really no more than a struggling actor who made believe. After turbulent days of wrestling with his conscience he musters up the courage to make a public confession on the steps of city hall, admitting that he is a fraud and Captain Avenger is just an imaginary character, like Santa Claus. The people of the city are terribly disheartened, they boo and jeer him, and our ex-hero mopes home with his head hung in ignominy, more discouraged than ever.

But because the darkest hour gives birth to the new day, so comes this hero's redemption. Walking home after his confession, he comes upon a flaming building surrounded by fire engines. As he looks up he sees a family trapped on the top floor, beyond where the firemen can reach with their ladder. The family's only hope is to jump into the net, but they are scared stiff. But not our hero. Fearlessly he scales a burning back staircase and rescues them all. Our hero-at-large turns out to be a large hero, for he did not give up and he was willing to go on stage one more time for one final act as Captain Avenger. This time, however, it was the stage of life.

The delightful teaching of the movie is that although the hero was at first just acting brave, he actually *was* brave. He really did have courage all along; it just took some practice for his strength to be brought forth. Like many of our lives, it took a crisis to draw his dormant potential out. Even though he gave up on himself, *the real hero in him never quit.* You see, it was the hero that was real, and the actor the imposter.

Captain Avenger is, of course, *us*. We are all heroes-at-large. We may not save people from robberies or burning buildings, but each of us has a hidden identity of courage that becomes obvious and powerful as soon as we are willing to remove our overcoats of self-consciousness and unworthiness. I have found some kind of greatness in every person I have ever known. Some are marvelous through brave deeds and many are magnificent through silent simplicity. A scattered few receive grandiose acclaim, while more find fulfillment in the quiet joys of inner satisfaction. Some are rewarded in seeing their name on a Broadway marquee, while others take delight in the giggle of a happy child. Or putting the finishing touch on a quiche. Or planting a magnolia. Or seeing another human being learning to love life. The ways of God's greatness are as plentiful as the stars of the heavens.

There is an idea with which I have been experimenting lately, one about which I am tremendously excited. It is the thought that to make a dream come true, it does not have to be a *probability* — it can just be a *possibility*. Possibilities are seeds. Whenever I feel I can't achieve something, I ask myself, "Is there one possibility — even *one* possibilty *in a million* — that this could really turn out right?" The answer must always be "Yes!" because anything is possible. If your chance of winning the lottery is one in twenty thousand, it is really a possibility; it is not zero — it is one. Somebody has to be that one, and it could just as well be you as the next person. That's how I've been thinking lately.

The most exciting change that has come with this way of thinking is that the moment I accept that possibility — even if it's one in a million — my whole feeling about the situation changes, and a tremendous surge of enthusiasm wells up in me. I actually begin to feel as if the idea has *already become a reality!* It is one of the most amazing transformations of consciousness I have ever experienced. It is accomplishing the quantum leap from one-in-a-million to "Yes!" That little one in a million opens up a wedge, makes a little hole in the dike, an opening that lets all the positive energy come through and makes the impossible possible. It's a fantastic way of thinking.

We just need to be able to see what we want, even before it comes around the corner. A few years ago three friends and I went to see *Meetings with Remarkable Men* in New York City. As we walked back to the bus station after the movie, it became increasingly clear that we would be late and our chances of making the bus were small. I gave up and began to walk more slowly. But my friends did not. "Come on!" they encouraged, "We can make it!" So we ran.

When we arrived at the terminal, one of our group went to buy the tickets while the rest of us dashed for the bus. As we got to the gate, the bus was just pulling out, and we flagged it down. The driver stopped to let us on, but that did not solve the problem of our tickets. I told the driver, "Our friend is downstairs getting our tickets . . . He'll be just a few minutes . . . Can you wait?"

"I'm sorry," the driver returned, "I have a schedule to meet and I'm late already . . . You'll have to wait until the next bus."

Disheartened, I accepted our failure (you can see why I have to practice positive thinking), and I began to step back off the big orange bus. Just then, one of the fellows with me, Paul, looked around the bend and shouted, "Here he comes!" After about twenty seconds our friend appeared, we all boarded the bus, and on our way we went.

I sat down next to Paul and breathed a sigh of relief. "Whew!" I let go, "It sure was great that you saw him when you did!"

"Do you want to know the truth?" Paul responded with a big grin. "I didn't see him when I said I did! I had no idea where he was or when he would come! I just said that to stall the bus driver, with my fingers crossed that he would show soon!"

"Faith," I declared to myself. Or trust. Or pretense. Or downright *chutzpah*. Whatever it was, it worked. As I pondered on what had actually happened, the lesson became clear to me that we have to have the nerve to believe that we are more than we think we are. We have to be willing to celebrate our own self coming around the bend before we can actually see it. We have to be willing to take a chance on ourselves making it. The only alternative is to wait until the next bus, and we often do not know when that will be. A friend of mine uses this motto:

WHEN YOU FORGET WHO YOU ARE
AND DON'T KNOW WHAT TO DO,
ACT THE WAY YOU WOULD IF YOU DID.

Psychologists tell us that our consciousness is like a huge iceberg with just a little tip showing, and most of it hidden in the subconscious. So it is with our *super*conscious — our higher self, our Divine Potential.

We have seen just a bit — a coming attraction of who we will be when we realize who we are. There was a song by The Band with the chorus, "*When you wake up you will remember everything,*" and this is what has already begun to happen. We are starting to wake up, and the morning light is revealing that we were sleeping in a palace, though we dreamed it was a hovel. While we thought we were abandoned to a bleak ruin, we are discovering that we are children of a King, and the entire kingdom is available to us because a father's greatest pleasure is to share his life with his children.

The time is now come for us to receive our destiny. The Divine Flame is sparkling within us, shining away the old shadows of who we, in a moment of forgetfulness, thought we were. I — and I believe you, as well — have been receiving glimpses, insights, flashes of what we can be when we allow God to work through us. Pictures and images are coming in dreams, in meditations, in quiet walks along the beach at sunset. They are coming through books, through music, through the voices of our brothers and sisters, through motion pictures. Stories like *Close Encounters of the Third Kind, E.T.*, the spiritual voyages of the Starship *Enterprise*, and Yoda's lessons of The Force are no accident; they are so enormously popular because the principles they depict are more spiritual truth than science fiction. These masterpieces contain deep teachings for the masses, lessons which are being given through the media as a way of reaching many persons rapidly and succinctly. In the old days you would have had to go to the Himalayas or a Hopi gathering or find an esoteric occult teacher to hear words of Truth. But now, because there is a quantum leap of consciousness stirring on this planet, God is working through the open minds of creative persons like Steven Spielberg and Gene Roddenberry to carry the message of the New Age to all who have ears to hear. In fact, The Force of Truth is eager to work through any person — like you and me — who asks to be a channel for it. Spielberg and Roddenberry have brought Truth to the masses because they have been willing to *listen* and *speak* through the medium of their talent. Many of us have been listening, but not speaking. Now is our time to speak. Through words. Through pottery. Through housecleaning. Through right business. Through silence. Through every avenue that our heart guides us to walk for the sake of creating a new world. Now is the time for the workers of Truth to come forth and make a stand for the Light. Now is the time.

RISING IN LOVE

When I was a child my heroes were always "out there." I had a Davy Crockett coonskin cap. I went to the record department of Korvette's to meet Chubby Checker and get his autograph on the back of a matchbook cover. The highlight of my fourteenth year was the night I saw a live Beatles concert in Atlantic City. (The screaming was so loud that I hardly heard a note of music, but it didn't really matter — I was in the same room with John, Paul, George, and Ringo!) Then I went home and played their songs on my guitar.

Later my musical heroes were replaced by spiritual guides. I put Ram Dass' picture up on my kitchen wall. I went to a mountain top in New Mexico to be with Patricia Sun. I bought a Yoda t-shirt. All because I wanted to know God, and I felt that these beautiful beings knew the One I sought.

Then my search carried me into a new light. As I absorbed the loving wisdom of these teachers, I began to see one common thread in all of their teachings:

LOOK WITHIN, AND THERE SHALL YOU FIND
THE TREASURE OF YOUR HEART'S YEARNING.

So I did, and I realized that their words were True. The hero for whom I was searching was *me*. All that I wanted from them, I could find within my very self, in the Light that God breathed into me. My searching came to an end when I was introduced to the one person in my life who could save me, and that was my Divine Self. Then I began to play my own songs on my guitar; I began to sing my own song.

The wondrous mystery of this self-discovery, this first hearing the tune of my own song, was that as I discovered the hero within myself I began to see the hero in everyone else, as well. I saw that each of us has our own song that only each of us can sing. I saw that when we fail it is simply because we do not realize that all that we seek is already within us, and when we succeed it is because we know that God believes in us enough to recreate Himself in us *as us*. It is said that *"There is nothing so powerful as an idea whose time has come."* When we remember who we are, we may rightfully add, *"There is no one so dynamic as a sleeping hero whose time has come to awaken."*

Growing Into Greatness

The Butterfly*

The innocent children discovered the killer sleeping in the hayloft. He had fled from the city where his crime was committed and taken refuge in the deserted barn. The children did not know of his misdeed.

"Who do you think he is?" the little girl asked her brother.

"I don't know . . . Who do you think he looks like?"

"Well, he has long hair and a beard."

"And he's about as old as daddy."

"He has sandals on."

"Maybe he's Jesus!"

"Do you think he could be?"

"Well, that's what the Sunday School teacher said Jesus looked like!"

"Yes! I'll bet it *is* him!"

"Oh, aren't we lucky to have Jesus — Gentle Jesus — come to our very own town!"

The killer, awakened by the exclamations, sat up, startled. He was about to flee when he heard the girl calling, "Jesus, Gentle Jesus, will you stay and play with us for a little while?"

"We will take care of you!" promised the little boy.

"Yes!" echoed his sister . . . "We will bring you food and blankets and we won't tell anyone you are here!"

"Oh please, Gentle Jesus, will you stay with us?"

The killer began to understand what was happening. He thought it over. It seemed like a safe bet, for a while at least. Yes, he would stay.

Over the next days and weeks, the children brought him food and clothing and even wine for him to bless. And with these things, they brought their innocent love and their adoration for the sweet and kind savior.

---

*This story is adapted from the plot of an old movie which was recounted to me, the title or author of which I do not know.

The killer felt safe with them, and the weeks turned into months. The children came to him every day and asked him to tell them parables and to bless them and their families.

So he did. As the summer went on, he actually began to enjoy playing the role of the Man of Peace. It was, of course, only an act, but there was something that felt good about it, something that he had not felt in many years, perhaps since he was a child and his grandmother would tell him stories of Jesus and the children.

As the man basked in the warm love of these children, he learned to love them, too. He began to look forward to the times when they would come, when he would tell them parables about the wonders of heaven's kingdom and the importance of loving our neighbors. One day he even found himself telling a parable that no one had ever heard, and this made the children so happy to hear a parable directly from their Gentle Jesus, one that was not even in the Bible.

The man's feelings about people, about the world, about life, began to soften, and he became gentle and kind. He read the Bible when he was alone, and something happened within him, something like a long-locked door opening to admit morning sunlight.

One evening he came upon the story of the prodigal son, and he began to weep. "Yes, this is the Truth," he thought to himself. In that moment he realized ever so clearly that it was *he* who was the prodigal son, and that he had sinned against man and God. He knew, too, that his soul could not be cleansed until he made restitution for his crime. So he decided to return to the city and confess.

The next time his beloved children came, he took them in his arms and drew them close to his breast.

"My dear ones," he quietly began, "it is now the time for me to leave you."

"But where are you going?" the little ones asked with tears streaming down their soft cheeks.

He gathered both of them closer to him and embraced them even more strongly.

"I must return to my Father," he explained, fighting back his own tears.

"Then we shall go with you!" they pleaded.

"No . . . Where I am going, you cannot come."

"But we want to know the Father, too."

"My dear ones, you already do know the Father . . . Did you not feel the peace in the long walks that we took through the meadow? . . . And did we not laugh with one another as we watched the little colts struggling to stand on their new legs? . . . And do you remember how we slept under the stars and awoke to the gentle cooing of the doves? If you know me, and if you have loved all that we have done together, you already know the Father."

"Then will you give us something to remember you by, Gentle Jesus?"

"I leave with you the gentleness that you have given to me. This is my peace that I give unto you."

And the son arose, and went unto his Father.

The Turning Point

The lowest ebb is the turn of the tide.

There is a turning point for every soul. It is the blessed moment when the hardships of life's adversity give way to the awakening to the presence of God. It is the hour of crisis which bears the child of Spirit. It is the end of suffering and the dawn of freedom. It is God's finest hour and the happy opportunity of Truth to shine into a dark life. It is the renaissance of all of us.

The awakening to light does not always come as an explosion, but more often at the end of a pendulum's swing, as the weight of worldly struggle yields to the understanding that there is a path of simplicity far easier than common ambition. At such a critical juncture in a soul's evolution, the Child of God has completed his journey into the nether world and set his foot back upon the way to his Father's home, now just a glimmer of hope in the distance, the only guiding star above a dark forest. And for such a soul in such a position, that glimmer is infinitely worth following.

But because we humans are among the most stubborn of creatures, our backs are often against the wall before we are willing to entertain the possibility that God's way is more joyful than the one we have adopted. We have learned to be willful and doubtful, and so we often refuse to consider God's design until ours has reached a dead end. Yet, because God is God, there She stands, patiently waiting for us with open arms, willing to accept us no matter how many dead end routes we have impudently trod. As Hilda once asked us, "Where else could you fall, but into the arms of God?"

A few nights ago I met a woman who experienced the death of her two-and-a-half year old son. She told me that this was her turning point, for it forced her to look at her life — and all of life — from a

41

broader, higher perspective. It turned her awareness toward God and, as she explained to me, "It gave me an entirely new and more purposeful direction in my life." As we discussed her experience, it appeared to me that she had come into great clarity about her trial. "It may sound strange," she went on, "but now I can't imagine him *not* passing on. I know that it had to be that way for the highest good of both of us."

That is the perspective at which we must all eventually arrive, each through our own struggles and challenges. In college I experienced a major turning point. One day I came to the stark realization that many of the things that I valued — money, power, sex, prestige, career, and possessions — were empty. It became so clear to me that all of these seeming treasures that I had spent much of my life pursuing as sources of security were essentially unstable and had no ability to shield or save me from life's changes. It was as if I was sitting in a movie theatre believing that everything I saw on the screen was real, when the lights in the theatre flashed on to completely erase all the forms on the screen. It was a startling and frightening disillusionment.

Following this jolt, I went through a kind of dark night of the soul, a feeling of emptiness in which everything I saw had no substance, no meaning, no reality. It was as if I was in a macabre amusement park where everything I touched crumbled to dust. I remember walking into the college cafeteria and seeing a book entitled *Nothingness*, and I figured this was the end of the line, the universe is a cosmic practical joke and we all end up in a big black hole. It is at this point of experience that many existential philosophers give up their quest for Truth and conclude that all is meaningless.

But because there is more to God than existentialism, She was right there to extend Her kind hand to help me to the other side of the chasm. She sent someone into my life who gave me a book called *Positive Disintegration*, by a psychologist named Dombrowski who said that going to pieces is sometimes the best thing that can happen to someone, for a life which is laboring under a false, painful belief system must be taken apart before a new and better one can be established in its place. What many people experience as nervous breakdowns or psychotic episodes are actually the soul's way of breaking out of a shell that once protected it, but now inhibits it. If we grew up in a family (or a world) where there was a great deal of negativity, emotional turbulence, or insensitivity, it was useful — and perhaps necessary — for us to build a protective shell around ourselves to shield us from the harshness of our environment. Our shielding systems serve us well as practical defenses against injury. (As I look at the hands that are writing now, I see they are calloused from the physical work I have been doing this summer. Because they have been exposed to continuous friction, the God-imbued intelligence of the body has built a tough layer of resilient tissue over the soft skin to protect and sustain it. When the autumn comes and that friction ceases, the callous areas will fall away and tender skin will be rebuilt with as much sensitivity as it originally enjoyed.) So it is with the journey of the soul through the seasons of life. Though a spiritual being must sometimes temporarily sacrifice its sensitivity and retreat to an inner shelter during the winter of adversity, there must come a spring when that tough shell is cracked to release the finer higher self from the cocoon and let it free to fly as it was originally intended.

A few weeks ago someone showed me some amazing flowers called peonies, lovely creations which bud forth in little round, hard balls. It was explained to me that by a miracle of nature the only way these buds can open is by means of certain little ants coming to eat away the outer shell. The flowers, you see, cannot open by themselves; their protection must be gnawed away by bugs. Then the most radiant, delicate, and colorful flowers emerge to celebrate the sunshine.

Those flowers and ants gave me a new appreciation for the gift that challenges bring to my awakening. They gave me a divine perspective on the aspects of my life that bug me. Just imagine: Every little bite the world takes out of my ego makes a bit more of an opening for the flower of the soul to emerge. Lesson of the peonies, number one.

Lesson number two: We can't do it by ourselves. We really need each other to rub off our rough edges. If we run away from challenges, we only prevent ourselves from growing. We may think we have escaped pain, but we have only resisted awakening. Pain does not come from a person or place or event; it is created in *the mind.* As long as we run from the thing that we resist, the pain stays in the mind. When we face the object of our difficulty, only then do we have an opportunity to free ourselves. Yes, there is a time when retreat and renewal are necessary, and it is sometimes very healthy to get away from it all to regroup. But there is also a time to courageously stand up to the monsters of the mind, the ones that turn out to be no more real than the big papier maché props they use in Hollywood, empty machines with no power except that which they are given by those who fear them.

The third gift of the peonies is the teaching that those monsters (sometimes just big bugs) come to us at *exactly* the moment we are ready to benefit from the strength we gain by learning to handle them. It is said that *we are never given a challenge beyond our ability to master*, and we might add that the arrival of those adversities is perfectly timed according to the stage of personal growth that we have attained; we get exactly what we need to advance us to the next level. The most intriguing aspect of the process of the peonies was that the ants — a special kind of ant — somehow appeared just at the moment that the flowers were ready to bloom. When I saw those little insects crawling about, having come from seemingly nowhere, all I could say was, "Amazing! . . . It's a miracle!"

This brings us to an idea that has helped me through many turning points: *God does not take anything away from us without giving us something better in its place.* There is never any loss without greater gain. If we want greater good to come into our life, we must make space for it. If we do not do it ourselves, God, who always works for our best interest, will make that opening for us — whether we like it or not. He'll get us fired from the job that no longer serves our highest good, to put us into one where we can better do His work. He'll break us up from our lover, so we can find a new and more fulfilling relationship. He'll close all doors except the one He wants us to walk through. In *Lost Horizon*, the disoriented travellers ask if the High Lama can find them guides to show the way home. "The High Lama," they are told, "arranges *everything*."

After going through my "emptiness period," my life became infinitely richer. You see, the emptiness was not the end, but a sort of clearing out time, a season for the roots of the old dead plants to disintegrate so the new seeds would have room to grow. In fact, my new life after that clearing out is so different than the old, that I hardly think of it as being a part of the same life, or of me as being the same person. The difference in the quality of my life is so striking that it is as if I was born anew. But only after the old was cleared away to "Prepare ye the way of the Lord."

We are now collectively going through such a clearing as a country, a society, a family of humankind. As we weather the tribulation now upon the earth, and that which is said to be coming, we must always remember that the peace that will come out of the hardship far outweighs the difficulties we experience. As we see idolized institutions like governments, schools, and monies fall by the wayside, we must know that this is happening only because they have too often not been conducted in the light of the high principles of Godly purpose upon which they were originally founded. These institutions must undergo a period of transformation after which they will be replaced by a new way of living that holds Divinity as its dearest value.

The earth as a whole has graduated to planetary consciousness. There is one huge turning point for the race of man, and it is now. There is no turning back. There is a maxim that *You are responsible for as much as you are aware* — no more, no less. The truth of this idea was brought home to me by a political analyst discussing the nuclear freeze and disarmament. He said, "Even if all of the nations on the earth were to completely dismantle all atomic weapons, that would not completely solve the problem, for, you see, as long as one person knows *how* to build them, there is the constant question of *'Will we use them?'* "

We are now ready to take another step, one of great responsibility. And that is wonderful, for as the oriental sage put it, *"Crisis equals danger plus opportunity."* As our old world crumbles around us, it is imperative that we do not become lost in thoughts of insecurity, fear, and confusion. The only way to deal with these changes is to expand our notion of what is being transformed around us, to include the understanding that great good always comes from the annihilation of unconsciousness and all of the things, acts, and events that unconsciousness breeds. There is a new, bright world waiting for us to claim it, and the knowledge that it is real is the saving grace that will bear us through the darkest night. We must keep our eyes and hearts focused on the light at the end of the tunnel and realize that the darkest hour is not only just before dawn, but it is the very promise that dawn is nigh. This high awareness, the vision that dissolution actually prepares the way of resurrection, is the shining star that guides us across the desert to the birthplace of the Christ. Thus does the last storm of winter moisten the earth for the first seeds of spring.

Bombshells to Songbells

And into plowshares shall the nations beat their swords.
— Isaiah 2:4

I closed my eyes and allowed the mystical tones of the Tibetan temple bells to play through my body. Each ancient sound vibrated gently, touching me in deeper and more subtle centers within myself. It was as if I was being lifted into meditation on the graceful echoing voices of a thousand chanting monks, drawing me to join them in consecration of the gift of sound. As the last tone rolled through the innermost recesses of my being, I gratefully savored its lingering sweetness.

"The sounds you have just heard are those of bullets," reported Job Matusow, the musician and storyteller *par excellence* who had just offered the concert. I could hardly believe my ears. Bullets?

"If you look closely at the bells," he explained, "you will notice that each of them is actually the shell of a tank or machine gun bullet, carefully reforged to produce the beautiful tones you just enjoyed."

I looked more closely. There must have been forty bullet shells, of all shapes and sizes. To my amazement, he was telling the truth. "How did he come to do this?" I marvelled, ". . . and why?"

"The concert you have heard is the realization of a dream I have had for many years," Job explained. "During World War II, I was stationed on the battle lines as a camp guard. Part of my job was to signal the troops. Out of necessity and lack of any other materials, we rigged up a few of these empty tank shells, which served the purpose well.

"It was during a night watch that I noticed how soft and soothing were the sounds of these bells. That night I made a vow that if I ever got out of the war alive I would collect some of these shells and turn instruments of destruction into vessels of God's peace.

"When I got home, by God's Grace, I contacted the government, which gave me the bullets you see before you now. I have since had the joy to play these bells for many groups — especially school children

47

and, most meaningfully, for an Easter morning ceremony on the deck of a docked U.S. Navy battleship."

Waves of enthusiasm rolled through me. What a lesson! "That's what I want to do with my life," I immediately felt, "— turn negatives into positives and serve God through the transformation."

I was given a golden opportunity to practice this lesson when one morning around 7 a.m. I was sitting in meditation, about to dive into a state of joyous bliss. Just at that moment my ears — and my whole body — were assaulted by a *THUMP—THUMP-THUMP . . . THUMP—THUMP-THUMP* from the other side of the wall, where dwelt an energetic twelve-year-old boy. Following this rude annuncia-tion came the sounds, *"ANOTHER ONE BITES THE DUST! . . . UNKH! — THUMP—THUMP-THUMP . . . ANOTHER ONE BITES THE DUST! . . . UNKH! . . . ANOTHER ONE GONE, ANOTHER ONE GONE, ANOTHER ONE BITES THE DUST! . . . THUMP—THUMP-THUMP . . . UNKH!"*

When I finally recovered my wits, I recognized these exotic sounds as a popular punk rock song, my neighbor's idea of a lively way to greet the new day. Unfortunately, it was not exactly my idea of a pleas-ant wake-up greeting, especially in the middle of a sweet etheric medita-tion. My first impulse was to jump up, pound on the wall, and yell to him, *"Turn that racket down!"* Either that or call the Environmental Protection Agency.

But then I remembered one of Hilda's practical lessons on turning every negative into a positive. She recounted that when she was stay-ing in San Francisco she lived right next to a cable car line that sent loud, motley noises through her window every time one of the street-cars passed her apartment. Realizing that there was nothing she could do to stop it, she decided to make something pleasant out of it. "You know what it reminded me of, kids?" she asked as she gathered us into her experience. "It sounded just like those nice tinkling oriental bells, the kind I used to hear in Ceylon. So every time that old cable car rattled by, I made believe I was in some quaint oriental village listening to an enchanting concert. You know, *'hing, bing . . . chung, chung . . . ta, hing.'* " (We always laugh whenever she gives her rendition of those bells; even though I must have heard the story a dozen times, every performance is delightful.) "That's what I suggest you kids do: Always find some way to turn a challenge into a blessing; all it requires is a bit of *imagination.*"

So there I sat at an unsolicited 7 a.m. disco, attempting to figure out some way to turn the new wave into the new age. For a while I sat there feeling agitated and confused, and then I hit on it: I would make believe that it was my *thoughts* that were biting the dust! "After all," I thought, "that's what meditation is all about, isn't it? — letting go of unwanted thoughts and letting them disintegrate!" So every time *"ANOTHER ONE BITES THE DUST!"* came around, I picked one thought I wanted to get rid of, and I made believe it had been knocked off. First there was my feeling insulted about something someone had said to me — *ANOTHER ONE BITES THE DUST — UNKH!* And then my confusion about what to do today — *ANOTHER ONE BITES THE DUST — UNKH!* And then my irritation at the kid who was playing the music — *ANOTHER ONE BITES THE DUST — UNKH!* And so on. Before long, it was really fun. You wouldn't believe all the thoughts that bit the dust that morning. It made war movies seem tranquil by comparison. By the time that record was over I had had a very excellent meditation indeed — perhaps one of the most practical. As I arose, I realized that the most fragrant incense is manufactured from the crudest punk.

The ability to turn minuses into pluses is a vital key to abundant living. People who have very little material goods are forced to develop this talent. I remember driving through a run-down section of New York City one night, looking at the broken buildings and shabby shops. Then I saw about half a dozen enthusiastic young guys enjoying a rousing game of basketball. I looked again and saw that there was no playground; they had discovered a hole in the awning of a shop, just about the size of a basketball hoop, just about the right height. They took what they had and made what they wanted.

And then there is my friend Jeff, whose mother's friend gave him an old 1962 Rambler for the legal fee of one dollar, with the tongue-in-cheek blessing that "You're lucky if you get six months out of this heap!" That was eight years ago. Jeff has given the car loving care, and it is doing fine. I know — I went to the movies in it yesterday.

Ingenius persons like these remind me again and again that *things are not good or bad in and of themselves, but it is what we make of them that determines their worth.* We have the power to mold all of life according to the direction we choose, and the way we look at our experiences is the pivotal factor that determines how it all turns out.

As Dr. Eric Butterworth has often said, "Our job is not to *set* things right; we simply need to *see* them right."

Years ago I learned this valuable lesson from my professor, Alfred Gorman, who taught us how to make the most of people working together in a group. Said Dr. Gorman, "Every group member, no matter how negatively they are acting or what a hindrance they may seem to be, is a potential real asset to the group. In fact, the more energy they are putting into being negative, the greater will be their contribution if you can just get them to channel their energy in a productive direction.

"Take the 'class clown' or practical joker, for example. Such a person has a need for attention and recognition. If they are not getting it, they will be a disruptive pest to the class. But, with a little positive attention and acknowledgement, they can cut their joking down to appropriate times and serve the very important function of a tension reliever.

"In the same way, the 'tough battler' — the one who challenges nearly every statement made by the other group members — can turn into a very good 'devil's advocate' and force the group to carefully examine its decisions. And the 'group mother' who tends to smother group members with over-support and unsolicited protection can be an extremely vital asset to the group during tough times, if she learns to give support where and when it is really needed. So, you see, there are really no destructive group members — only misdirected uses of energy. In the final analysis, *all* group members can serve an important positive function."

Because Truth must be true on all levels, these principles apply not only to encounter groups and classrooms, but to all of life. I have been shown that in organic gardening, for example, most insects serve a necessary function. When you upset the balance by removing some ladybugs, you find that the bugs they were eating become a bigger problem. So the "enemies" you removed were actually your good friends. Although Jesus didn't use the term "organic gardening," he did say, "*Love your enemies, bless those that curse you, and pray for those who spitefully use you.*"

A friend of mine gave me a very helpful insight into the deeper meaning of "loving your enemies." He said that we might look at the enemies *within* ourselves — the bad habits and traits that we don't like about ourselves — as the enemies that we must learn to love. It seems that the more we fight our shortcomings — overeating, smoking, or lack of emotional control, for example — the more they fight back, often with hidden weapons (like dreams of Häagen-Dazs banana splits). It is said that *"What we resist, expands and persists,"* and this is why brute resistance (against a person or a trait) only adds fuel to the problem. The subtle secret of conquering our inner enemies is to stop hating and fighting them, and start appreciating them for what they can offer to our personal and spiritual growth.

In the last New York Marathon there was a runner who, at the age of thirty, had weighed 300 pounds, smoked four packs of cigarettes a day, and had gone through a series of heart operations. One day, however, he got sick and tired of being sick and tired, and he decided to make his life work *for* him, and not against his best interests. So he quit smoking, cleaned up his diet, lost 140 pounds, and when I saw him he was running the marathon with a smile on his face.

This man *used* his bad habits as a springboard to develop the strengths of self-control, determination, and good health. Perhaps these were the qualities that he needed to cultivate in this life, and his soul purposely took on these harmful habits as a focal point for learning how to overcome them. In order to develop tremendous discipline, he had to have a formidable obstacle. The armed forces train soldiers on rigorous obstacle courses, designed to force infantrymen to become very strong for battle. Though the new soldiers may curse the objects they have to surmount, when the battle comes they look back and bless them. Though we may not face physical warfare, we are all warriors of life; as Don Juan told Carlos Castenada, we must all be *impeccable warriors*, at that. Then, when we have learned how to remain peaceful in the face of even the most difficult times, we will look back on all the little challenges that barbed us and through which we grew strong through overcoming, and bless them.

It is exactly this kind of transformation through overcoming unwanted habits that enables us to eventually uplift one another. The most powerful healers and change agents are those who have grown through a tremendous difficulty and then brought the benefit of their experience to help others going through the predicament that they have mastered. I know a man who healed his cancer through meditation and went on to teach thousands of other persons to do the same. You will probably recognize, too, that the most successful therapeutic organizations, such as Alcoholics Anonymous and Weight Watchers, are built on the strength of people who have conquered their temptation and gladly share their victory with those who are still in the process of conquering. Such persons have balanced themselves against the desires that used to drag them down (like a jogger doing isometric exercises), and used that power to bolster the spiritual muscles necessary for real self-transformation. In such a case, the old "enemies" were actually friends in disguise; we just needed to learn how to relate to them to make them work for us. Then, after we have become a more integrated person through mastering those old traits, we can "bless those (habits) that spitefully used you," for, like a mountain climber who finds a heap of rocks at the bottom of a sharp slope and then rearranges them as steppingstones upward, we can see that the elements of the situation were not bad at all — we just had to fit them into their right place.

Once again we find that all is God. This is the first lesson, and the last. Our job is to discover God in that which we judged to be ungodly, to find the good where others see evil, to see the Mary in the Magdalene. This means that there *must* be unity in what now seems to be alienation, saintliness where sinners now stand, and Love in the midst of bitterness. Put more simply, there is hope for all of us and all of life, and that is the great truth that keeps God loving us. Perhaps He hears the songbells in our souls.

> *I believe that God is in*
> *   me*
> *as the sun is in the*
> *   rainbow,*
> *the light in my*
> *   darkness*
> *the voice in my*
> *   silence.*

> — Helen Keller

Lifting The Past Into Love

I release all of my past to the Light.
— The Light Prayer

It seems that just when we have made up our mind to step forward into a new future, the past comes back to haunt us. The moment we decide we want to clean up our life, old dirt bubbles up like sludge from a stuffy drain. Just when we declare our intention to quit smoking pot, or let go of promiscuity, or stop working late on Thursday night so we can go to meditation class, almost immediately we receive a flurry of invitations to a big party where there is guaranteed to be "the best Columbian," or we hear from the guy we met last year who was living with someone, but now he just broke up with his girlfriend, or the boss calls us into his office to ask the special favor of working overtime this Thursday night. Such a time is a trying and challenging period for the spiritual aspirant, for it seems as if "I'll never get rid of my negative past."

But this is exactly the time to push on with determination. Such a period of facing the unwanted past is a time of *testing*, and the way to pass the tests is to realize that we really can have the future for which we yearn, if we just put up with this "return mail" for a while. As we begin to see these trials for what they are, they become much more bearable and more quickly and easily overcome. Such challenges are golden opportunities to become strong by mobilizing faith, firmly planting our feet on solid spiritual ground, and making a dynamic stand for the Truth. These tests are, in fact, gifts from God, and if we know how to handle them properly, the energy we gain from overcoming them will catapult us into exhilirating spiritual freedom.

Let's take a deeper look at the dynamics of facing our past masterfully. Every thought we think, word we speak, and act we do creates reactions in the universe, like ripples emanating from a stone thrown into the center of a calm lake, ripples that eventually return to us in the form of waves — motions that *we* have created. We can be assured that every stone we have thrown will create waves; just because we haven't felt the waves yet doesn't mean that the stone just plunked in the water and nothing happened; it means that the waves haven't arrived *yet*. So we shouldn't be surprised when an old stone that we cast long ago comes back to affect us weeks, years, or lifetimes later; that's the law of physics, *karma*, and the entire universe.

Now imagine that you're getting tired of being sprayed (maybe drenched) by waves, and you start to see there is a relationship between your throwing heavy stones and your getting wet. So you decide not to throw any more boulders, which is a right decision. That will keep you from creating any new deluges, but it will not stop the waves that are already in motion from the stones you cast in the past.

That's exactly what the unwanted invitations to pot parties, old boyfriends, and working overtime are: waves that we have created, now breaking on the shore of our experience. This is actually cause for rejoicing, for *the waves disappear after they break on the shore*, and we are free of them. Then we can enjoy the picturesque patterns of ripples from the kind of stones we *choose* to cast, along with the cool water lapping over our feet at sunset. This is why it is of the *utmost importance not to despair* or say, "Well, it looks like I'll never be rid of that scene, so I might as well go along with it." We *will* be free of it — as long as we do not throw any new boulders.

Let's consider a very practical example: relationships. "Relationships" is a subject on the syllabus of the course called "Growing Through Life," on which most of us have been tested. Sometimes we have passed, and sometimes we have failed, but always we have learned. There was a time in my life when I was going out with several different women at one time. One of my college professors called this "multiple meaningful relationships." Whatever we call it, it was not long before I realized that all I was creating was multiple meaningful difficulties. One day I awoke to the fact that in these diluted relationships I was not really serving myself or any of these women, and it became clear to me that I would have to settle down.

So I made up my mind to commit myself to working sincerely on one relationship. As I did so, I knew that I had made the correct decision, for my emotions and my relationship and my life began to feel very clean, clear, and light. Ah! but just because I quit throwing many stones did not mean that I could escape the waves created by the stones

I had already cast. All at once I began to receive letters and phone calls from women I had met in the past, women with whom I had had some kind of flirtation, even very subtle, like, "If you're ever in New Jersey, say hello," or "Gee, you have nice eyes," or "If you ever break up with your boyfriend, look me up." (The last one's not so subtle, I guess.) As this flurry of old karma began to roll my way, I realized all too clearly that every action we generate in the universe is answered by an equal and opposite reaction. I felt like a racquetball player who had paddled out a lot of wild shots in a small court with no way for the balls to fly but back to where they were hit.

So I had to field them. I had to face every little flirtation I had initiated. I had started something, and I had to finish it out in the best way I could. Figuring out how to handle each situation was a tough one for me; I had to work each relationship out individually. Sometimes it meant accepting the invitation to come over and listen to some music, and then saying "Good night" after the last chord; sometimes it meant sitting down with the person and really sharing our honest feelings with each other until we had transformed our separateness into a holy communion of souls; and sometimes it required a firm "No, thank you — I'm not going to pot parties these days."

I discovered that there was no one way out; all I knew was that I wanted out, and because I was sincere in my aspiration, God told me what to say and do in each particular circumstance, a right action that was good for everyone involved. That's the miracle of God's compassion: we can really mess up, but if we sincerely resolve that we want a better life, He is right there with just the helping hand we need. Thank you, God.

Eventually my aspiration for a new way of relating to others became a reality. It didn't come easily and it didn't come immediately, but it came, and my life is the richer for it. *Patience*, I have found, is a key ingredient in this game. We get a taste of the Truth and we want to be liberated immediately, which is great, but we have to work within the flow of the universe. We can burn ourselves out if we try to change too quickly. I heard of one young man who literally killed himself from following too strict a spiritual regimen. This was not necessary, and neither was it spiritual. We have to trust that God will hear our prayer for change, and She will help us with it as fast as we can go. We just need to know that once we make up our mind about what we want for ourselves, it will come — It has to.

This brings us to the importance of forgiveness. We have to know that no matter how sordid or evil are the things that we have done, even if it seems that our whole life up to now has been one big mistake, God is willing to forgive us. Condemnation is not an idea from God — it is an invention of the human mind. God is willing to forgive *anything*. Some of the most saintly, holy people I know have been prostitutes, alcoholics, thieves, and outright arrogant sinners (you see the kind of crowd I hang out with — and I count myself among them). But all of our pasts are completely meaningless now. It is as if the light of God's forgiving love has dried up the old scabs and replaced them with brand new baby-like skin. As I get to know more and more beautiful people in the spiritual domain, I see that hardly any of them, like myself, are without some kind of worldly taint in their past. But, ah, though the world may record error, the soul stands ever shining and brilliant as the day it was breathed forth from God with Her commitment to love us forever, no matter what. No matter what.

I want to explain now why I don't believe in eternal damnation. First of all, nothing in the universe is eternal except God. As King Solomon taught, "This, too, shall pass." Everything comes and goes; all the things that I thought would last forever — my first girlfriend, the Yankees winning the World Series every year, my last girlfriend — all turned out to be temporary. The only thing that really endures is God, which is a pretty good deal because if I had to make a choice between my past being eternal or God's forgiveness being eternal, God is the winner by a huge margin.

Second, I can't imagine God allowing any of His Beloved Children (you and me and all of us), *created in His image and likeness,* to suffer everlasting pain. That means that God would breathe life and love into part of Himself and then condemn it to endless torment. That just doesn't make sense to me. What God would create a child that had to suffer through eternity? I believe God is smarter than that. I believe He knows His business, and He allows us only as much pain as we have brought upon ourselves to learn a lesson. The purpose of painful lessons is to guide us home to know the joy of spiritual freedom, to learn that pain is not necessary or even real. Once the lesson is learned, there is *absolutely no purpose* to further hardship. We may go through hellish experiences, but so far none of them have lasted forever, and I don't think pain will suddenly become eternal now. As Ram Dass says, "While you're going through travail it may seem like it will never end, but it will; you just went through eternal damnation for a little while." God is not a sadist. Even the meanest school teacher in the world would not keep a child after school forever. The teacher wants to get home and have dinner, and that's the end of the game. God may sometimes be tough, but He's not mean.

Any God that is genius enough to create a miracle-filled universe must be clever and loving enough not to throw part of Himself into hell forever. To the contrary, it seems only fitting that such a magnificent mind would recreate Himself in the form of children who could share His eternal joy. I mean, if you were God (which we are, created in His likeness), and you could create anything you wanted (which we can, through God's infinite energy), wouldn't you create something dynamically heavenly? I think so. If we earthlings would want to create something that beautiful, just think how much more glorious must be the designs of the Father of the Universe, the Lord of All Creation, The King of the Cosmos? I tell you, His plan is a real hum-dinger, one that even Steven Spielberg would approve.

We need to quit whipping ourselves — or believing that we deserve to be whipped — and start to say "Yes!" to a great big idea of forgiveness, bigger perhaps than we were taught as children. We are like people who have been imprisoned for so long that we don't even believe that freedom exists. When the Children of Israel were presented with their freedom from bondage in Egypt, a lot of them didn't know what to do with it; some of them even wanted to stay in Egypt, for the life of slavery was familiar and ironically more comfortable than their newfound freedom. But that won't really do. We have to accept our freedom. We have to march out of Egypt. We have to cross the Red Sea. We have to enter the Promised Land. Even if the waters seem high now, it might be a good idea to keep our seats until the last frame of the movie; you never know — something very interesting could happen when we reach the shore.

Our past does *not* have to haunt us forever. If we just put up with it for a while, the old patterns will wear themselves out for lack of repetition to sustain them. We must bless every opportunity to say "No!" to an old, unwanted pattern, for every "No!" to the old is a "Yes!" to the new. We sowed many seeds, some of them flowers and some of them weeds. Even if we do not plant any more weeds, we must wait for the old weed seeds to sprout before we can uproot them. That's why we have to be joyfully persistent in working toward our new ideals and leaving the old behind. Sometimes it takes just one good "No!" and sometimes it takes a hundred, but always the past must yield to a new and freer life.

Our history is not our destiny. I know God wants more for me than I used to want for myself. If my past ever starts to get me down, I just think of how good it would be if my desired future were real, and that vision gives me the confidence to persist until God triumphs.

Flowing Robes and Flannel Shirts

'Tis a gift to be simple, 'tis a gift to be free.
> — Shaker hymn

I met Susan on a weekend retreat in the mountains of Pennsylvania. She came over to the dining room table where I was sitting and asked if she could attend my yoga class with an injured knee. As we sat and talked before a great picture window looking onto the glorious autumn forest, I began to feel that our meeting was planned, destined by a design grander than I could explain. As I close my eyes now, I can so warmly feel the perfection of that scene, the morning sunlight dancing off Susan's face like sparkling angels playing on a mountain lake. Though I had just met her, I knew that Susan believed in God and in goodness and in healing, and I understood, too, that this was her moment. We placed our hands on her knee and as we did, both of us felt waves of healing energy streaming through our hands and her leg. It was one of the golden moments when life is lifted to its highest possibilities, and the reality of God is so obvious that you wonder how you ever could have forgotten it.

After the weekend, Susan and I began to correspond with one another. She would write of how her knee was improving and she told me of her life, her enthusiasms, her trials, and the peaks and valleys of her journey through personal growth. I returned with similar notes, offering suggestions for how she might deal with her challenges. We developed a nice friendship, getting to know one another as sort of spiritual pen-pals.

When I next saw Susan at a later retreat, something was not right. I could tell that she was feeling out of balance, and when I asked her about it she recoiled, unwilling to discuss what was bothering her. I tried to give her space to work out whatever she was going through, but the awkwardness of our communication was too weighty for me to ignore. (There is a story about a family who finds a bleeding

59

rhinoceros head on their table just before a dinner party, and they do not know what to do about it, so they decide to just leave it there, say nothing about it, and hope their guests will not notice it.) In our next group meeting I had to ask Susan what was bothering her.

"Well, to tell you the truth," she explained, "I've been having some hassles with my family, but I didn't want to tell you because I was afraid you would think I am not spiritual."

That really startled me. "But why?" I needed to know.

"Because I have this image of you as this really high, pure, spiritual teacher, and I felt that you might be put off by the worldliness of my problems."

When Susan said that, I began to get this empty, queezy feeling in the pit of my stomach, the kind you feel when you think you got an "A" on an exam and it comes back with a "45" on it. I felt that I had really missed the mark somewhere — and I had. That moment I realized that it was not just Susan's problem that she perceived me that way, but on some level I had fostered or encouraged that image of me. I saw that there was a part of me that wanted to be seen or known as some great, wise, all-knowing, transcendental, mystical Guru with all the answers for his many disciples. When I realized the effect that my liking that image had on my relationship with Susan, I felt like I had not only missed the mark, but the whole target as well.

I realized that I had allowed my relationship with Susan to fall into a phony pattern created by an idea of her as a questioning aspirant and me as an answering teacher. Patterns and games in our relationships are very easy, for they allow our roles to be well-defined and we are not required to deal with change or face our inner tender spots. But the awful price we pay is that we give up our aliveness and our genuineness, and we remain stuck in little narrow labyrinths like rats in a maze who get a little nibble of processed *Velveeta* at the dead end of each corridor, but remain starving for the real big cheese just on the other side of the wall that we are afraid to climb over. That's exactly the way I felt with Susan, like I had sold my soul for a pasted guru's beard and rented robes. It felt cheap and empty and I knew I didn't want it.

When I thought about how I really *did* want to relate to Susan, it was to be a friend, someone with whom she could feel comfortable and easy. I didn't want to be a guru sermonizing to her from behind a mahogany lectern, but someone who she could trust not to judge her. This led me to the self-discovery that I want to be an available and reachable person, without any false facades to distort the truth of our mutual holiness. I want to have no pretenses with you, for your love is very precious to me and your trust is infinitely more important to me than any image that would make me seem to be something I am not.

Susan's honesty in sharing her feelings helped me to become aware that I do not want to have to have all the answers all the time for everyone else; before I can even begin to serve another, I must find the light within myself. I want the freedom to grow, to change, not to be the same person I was yesterday, to be richly human. I would rather be a happy nobody than a miserable somebody. If I try to be a Ram Dass or Hilda or Swami Satchidananda, I am untrue to myself; the only way to fulfill my destiny is to be *me*. As I began to hear the melody of my own song, I knew that is exactly the one that God wants me to sing.

And wow, did that awareness feel good! As I readjusted who I could allow myself to be, I felt so light and happy, as if I had been relieved of a heavy burden — one of my own making. The priest's robe and collar that I had chosen were not made of cloth, but of binding steel, and letting go of them allowed me to be reborn as an innocent child. I traded in my rented robes for a flannel shirt and blue jeans, and replaced my congregation with a family of brothers and sisters. It was like walking out of a self-created prison into a verdant, fragrant meadow. It was discovering the freedom that I had never lost, only covered over and temporarily forgotten. It was coming home.

This realization led in turn to another: In my wanting to be Susan's teacher in that way, I was not only limiting myself, but also doing her an equally harmful disservice. I was demeaning her wholeness as a rich, complete person. In order for me to be above her, she had to be below me, and that is like robbing her Godhood from her, denying that she has a direct and complete connection with God through her very own heart. And in her willingness to have me as a guru, she lessened herself. As psychologist Sheldon Kopp says, "If you want someone else to be your guru, look again — you have diminished yourself." Because we are all one, when we cheat ourselves, we cheat all of us.

Then I understood why Ram Dass has called his recent lecture series "Nothing New from Nobody Special." For many years Ram Dass had an image of being a guru, a folk hero, a wise man. That's a horrible mold for a human being to live up to, for it creates an irreconcilable separation with everyone else, who automatically becomes an un-hero. The only way the game works in the long run is if we all get to be everything. We must all be equally heroes and sinners, gurus and disciples, teachers and students. If we lean too far in one direction, we tip the scales and throw our organism off kilter. Then we have to swing the other way to balance things out. That's why Ram Dass now has to be "Nobody Special" — because for a long time he was "Somebody Special." After all of the images are reconciled, all he will be is *free*, which he, like the rest of us, already is.

This is the keynote of this bright New Age that is dawning. We are all going to be each other's teachers — indeed we already are. All of us are going to be equally gurus and non-gurus. We must learn to recognize love in *all* of its forms. I believe that the days of turned-up collars and ochre robes and special seats in the synagogue are merging into a unity that honors *everyone* as holy. Those marks of reverence are expanding to include rolled-up sleeves and solar-heated homes and prayer meetings in which we all take turns reading from and explaining the holy books. No longer shall we blaspheme our real identity by looking to wise men for direction, but we shall all know that there is one Guru — the living God — who is willing to quicken the hearts and speak through the lips of all who dedicate themselves to the Light. While many today call themselves "guru," there is one sure way to distinguish the real ones from the charlatans: the real gurus say, "Be your own Guru, for God lives within you as you."

My own experience is the only subject on which I can write with honesty. As I now consider how free it felt to shed my robes and don my flannel shirt for the sake of healing my friendship with Susan, I remember a picture I saw in a high school English book, captioned, "*Mahatma Gandhi's possessions at the time of his death.*" There was a Bible, a pair of sandals, and eyeglasses. That was all. This man who led an entire nation to freedom did so on the strength of truth and simplicity alone. He won the hearts of even his staunchest opponents, who had to respect him because he depended solely on God. It seems to me that if one man such as Gandhi can conquer life without any pretenses, so can anyone. If we can just trust God enough to let go of who we think we have to be before we can be ourselves, we will find that the greatest gift that God has given us is who we already are.

Tough Love
(Ruthless Compassion)

*Sometimes, kids, it's cruel to be kind, and sometimes
it's kind to be cruel. You have to know which is which.*
— Hilda

One day in the supermarket I saw a friend of mine who had been having a hard time with her sixteen-year-old daughter. The girl was acting impudent, undisciplined, and spending a lot of time with a group of kids who were getting into trouble. "How is your daughter doing, Mrs. Dougherty?" I inquired.

"Oh, I must tell you what has happened," she offered. "Things have changed dramatically! My husband and I read a book called *Tough Love*, in which the author explains that a firm, consistent policy of discipline is sometimes the most loving gift a parent can offer a child. So now we have set limits on what she can do, and no matter how much she hoots or hollers or tells us she hates us, we hold our ground. And do you know what? It's working! I don't know why we didn't do this from the start!"

Tough love. God is the toughest lover of all. We may be tempted to rail against God when we feel that the universe has dealt us an unjust blow, but the trying times are the very moments when God is giving us the grace of learning how to return to the Home against which we have turned our back. The prodigal son wandered off into the far country, only to be forced back home by a famine which fell upon the land. Had the famine not come, he might have continued to wander in vain. The famine was cruel, yet mercifully kind.

I learned about tough love when I was in a relationship with a woman, a relationship in which I felt very attached and needy. It seemed that when she was affectionate to me I felt good, and when she acted cold I felt hurt. My happiness was almost completely dependent on the way she acted toward me. It was a fool's happiness; I had given her power over my peace of mind, a surrender which is never justified.

I remember several occasions when we were deciding whether or not to go our separate ways (a decision we made every few weeks). It was as if my soul had a choice: I could either let go or keep clinging. A still, small voice within me whispered, "It's O.K. to let go," while a thunderous band of roving desires shouted, "You must hang on!" When we would decide to stay together I got a rush of happiness, but it was empty, like a compulsive gambler who hits on a winning number but knows that it will not be long before he is again at the mercy of the loan sharks. The most honest thing I felt was not that I wanted to be with her, but that I was afraid not to be with her. I was just postponing the pain of separating that I anticipated, which is a pretty flimsy foundation upon which to build a human relationship.

When we finally did part, my experience was the exact reverse of my clinging: it hurt on the outside, but deep within me I knew that this particular relationship was not right from the start, and this ending was the best thing that could have happened to me. Looking back now, I see that the promptings of my soul were true. Tough love.

Tough love is what is required to break a habit that is working against our highest interests. When we do not take the proper steps that lead us up the path of our personal good, God steps in and says, "Let me handle this for you!" Like an alcoholic who takes "just one more for the road," we only strengthen our bondage by fulfilling desires that drag us into further hardship. Then God, or life, or the universe — whatever we prefer to call it — sooner or later turns us around by *not* giving us what we *think* we want, but what we *need*. Ken Keyes, author of the beautiful *Handbook to Higher Consciousness**, describes it this way: "When you have an addiction (any emotion-backed desire) and you satisfy it, you are not solving anything; you are only setting yourself up for the next problem." As the Rolling Stones put it, "You can't always get what you want, but if you try sometimes you just might find that you get what you need."

A good example of this principle is my friend Preston, who was extremely anxious about his job. He developed an ulcer, he could hardly sleep at night, and his uptightness began to be a hassle for his family and friends. He did not even really like the work; his inner self was

---

*Ken Keyes, Jr., *Handbook to Higher Consciousness*, Living Love Books, 1975.

longing to work in some kind of service or healing profession. But fear kept him clinging tenaciously to this job, at no matter what cost. Then, by God's Grace, he was fired. Preston went through some emotional turbulence for a little while and then, after he had gotten back on his feet, he went out and studied *shiatsu* — oriental massage therapy. At the age of thirty he went back to school, took the necessary coursework, and now he is a very satisfied and successful *shiatsu* therapist. Last week he told me, "I thank God every day that I was fired from that job. God took care of what I didn't have the guts to do. It was the best thing that ever happened to me."

We do not have to get fired, divorced, or ill to experience the grace of God's tough love. He is very happy to shake us up where we are, in the little experiences of everyday life. The universe is designed to support whatever harmonizes with it, and straighten out whoever is out of the flow. When I was in college I had a mad desire to buy a red Mustang GT fastback, which I went out and did — with money I didn't have. The purpose of the car was 10% transportation and 90% prestige; I just wanted people (namely female people) to see me driving around in it. I customized it, polished it, and purposely ran down six flights of stairs to move it to the spot in front of the dormitory where everyone could see it. You might say I was attached to it.

About a month after I bought the car I drove it to Boston to visit a friend for a weekend. When I went to "peel out" on Sunday afternoon, valise in hand, the car wasn't there. I must have paced up and down that street twenty times, my jaw dropping farther with each frantic step. But it wasn't there. Three days later my friend called and told me the Boston Police had found it in a run-down section of town. "Don't even bother to come and look at it," he told me, "unless you like looking at empty Ford chassis." My flashy car was stripped bare.

I am starting to see that this is what much of life is about — teaching us to get back to what we really need, instead of what we *think* we need. The hardships of life are God's way of stripping away our frivolous accessories until we are satisfied with the basic model, which is pretty much the way God wants us, for the sake of our own happiness. As the Talmudic sages remind us, we come into this world naked and we leave it naked, and everything else in between is excess baggage, most of which we would be better off without. It's as if God is always inviting us to return to the Garden of Eden, but in order to enter we have to slip through a narrow gate which will not allow for any extras. Sooner or later we realize that the no-frills brand is pretty much the same as the fancy-labeled product; when we go for the flashy items, we pay more for the name and the packaging. Deluded into thinking that we really *need* our new stereo, or our special meditation cushion, or nuclear power, we try to convince ourselves and God that we can bring our entourage into the Garden if we just slip in sideways or twist the scriptures slightly. When that doesn't work, we may try to sneak in by disguising ourselves as someone else, or by walking in backwards, or like Wile E. Coyote endlessly chasing Road Runner, we devise elaborate devices to catapult us over the Garden hedges. But when the smoke has cleared, there we sit, chin in hand, no closer to Heaven than we were before. The only way to do it is to really do it — no compromises, no plea bargaining, no "twofers." The world, life, and the universe are sometimes so tough because part of their purpose is to sandpaper our rough edges, to trim down that spiritual cellulite that stops us from fitting through the gate. All of our trials, disillusionments, and sufferings are part of a universal plot of great Love to slim down our metaphysical chubbiness, to get us into divine shape in a great reducing plan that makes Jack La Lanne's seem like kindergarten by comparison.

That's where discipline comes in. The rule of the Cosmic Spa membership is very simple: If we don't get our act together for ourselves, God will do everything in His power (and that's a lot of power) to do it for us. There's no way to escape life without learning some discipline. That's a rough one for those of us who grew up in the free fifties and the swinging sixties. I personally did not know what discipline was until I was fifteen years old, when my tenth-grade gym teacher told me that my push-ups were not much more than symbolic dips, and I had better shape up. For the first time I had some inkling that if I didn't toe the line, I'd have to pay the piper. Then I got to see that if you don't pay the piper when he presents his bill, you have to pay later — with interest.

Hilda, in her own inimitable way, taught us this lesson one holiday weekend when I and several families were together. A couple of little children began running through the gathering of adults, making a lot of disruptive noise. "Children!" Hilda reprimanded, "You must not run and shout like that in here . . . You may sit nicely with us if you like, or go into your room and play, but this is a quiet area for now." As the kids left the room, Hilda explained to us, "You must train

the children at an early age, or else you will have big problems later
. . . You don't want them to grow up like you, do you?"

We all had to laugh; we knew exactly what Hilda was talking
about. Many of us were raised in the age of permissiveness, when there
was a popular idea that if you just let kids do what they felt like doing,
they would eventually turn out O.K. Well, somehow many of us made
it, but I have a feeling it was not by method, but Grace. I can think
of too many instances (such as when I got caught walking out of an
Arab hotel with one of their towels, and the manager started to call
the police on Alan *Cohen*) that I was saved by a higher power than
I knew. As Hilda has said, "I'll bet your guardian angels must have grey
hair by now!"

We can save our guardian angels — and ourselves — some trouble by appreciating the value of tough love and applying it to ourselves
before God has to. The miracle of discipline is that it really is good
for us, and it feels good, and it works. I know that when I get into
a routine of doing yoga or jogging regularly, I realize how positively
it carries me through my entire day, and I really enjoy keeping with
it. Self-mastery is absolutely necessary for any kind of success in life.
Without discipline, self-control, and self-responsibility we are, to put
it in the vernacular, *blobs*. Every great artist, musician, or athlete has
gotten where he or she is only through long, arduous hours of practice. (As one insightful thinker has put it, "Success is 10% inspiration
and 90% *perspiration*.") It is a pipe dream to imagine that greatness
floats to us as a gift from the air. We have to earn it. I saw a beautiful
poster of a charming ballerina in an exquisitely graceful pose, the kind
that bore the mark of years of dedicated practice. The caption of the
photo was, "*Greatness is born of the marriage of skill and inspiration.*"
God plants within us the seeds of talent, but it is up to us to train our
mind, body and emotions to be worthy vessels through which He can
pour inspiration into expression. Only after we have brought our in-
strument into fine tuning and mastered the difficult sections of the sym-
phony can God whisper to us the phrasing that brings the audience
to tears.

This is the formula for unified godliness in action. Our Heavenly
Father created us to know the majestic wonders that life lives to teach
us, but Truth can offer us only as much awakening as we are strong
enough to accept. The moments of newfound freedom are made even
more precious by the rigor and perseverence that brought us to them.

RISING IN LOVE

A mountain lake at sunset is a picture of gentle tranquility, yet its gift of peace is indebted to the strength of the mountains that give it form. Sometimes love is gentle and sometimes love is, of necessity, tough. In the end, love must be everything, else love it would not be. Perhaps the realization that love can take the form of an unflinching disciplinarian is exactly the awareness we need to carry us through the hard times when it seems that love has abandoned us. Tough love is a gift from God that makes us who we want to be, but have not yet become because we thought we were less than we are. The truth of growth through challenge is the answer that makes whole our understanding that we chose to come to this rich, wondrous, and awesome planet certainly to love, and necessarily to learn.

Living In Light

Going For It

Only those who risk going too far can possibly find out how far one can go.

— T.S. Elliot

"Who do you think we can get to serve as the master of ceremonies for our dance recital?" asked Hilda's friend as the two pondered in an artfully decorated studio sometime in the 1940's.

"How about Ingrid Bergman?" Hilda replied.

"Ingrid Bergman?! Don't be silly . . . She's the hottest star in Hollywood! . . . Why should *she* want to come to *our* amateur production?"

"Why shouldn't she? . . . She might say 'Yes,' you know . . . It can't hurt to ask!"

"Well, alright," agreed Hilda's colleague. "If you want to try, go right ahead."

So Hilda went right ahead, and (as you may have guessed) when Hilda went on stage for her recital that night, she was introduced by: Miss Ingrid Bergman.

Yes, it can't hurt to ask. We miss out on much of what life has to offer, not because the things we long for are unattainable, but because we do not ask for them. Our problem is not that God withholds from us what we desire, but that we do not really expect Him to give it. Our growing into greatness is not a matter of rearranging the world around us, but of expanding the magnitude of our expectations to embrace the thrill of the possible. The road to freedom is paved with the anticipation of the miraculous.

One night Hilda told us, "God does not limit you; *you* limit *God*." That really hit home with me. It means that all of the boxes that we may feel restricted by — money, age, health, work, people — are not imposed by God, but by our thinking in terms of lack. This is a stunning realization, for with the understanding that we have bound ourselves comes the awakening that it is *we* who can free ourselves. We can quit thinking of ourselves as human, and start knowing ourselves as Divine.

I have discovered a way of breaking out of self-imposed molds. Whenever I have tried this experiment, it has changed my outlook on my life, and I would like to share it with you. The method is to:

GO FOR THE BEST.

Going for the best means to aim for what you really want, including — and especially — trying to do things that you think there's no way in the world you can do. For example: send an application for the job that only one woman in a hundred will get; call up the most beautiful girl in the class for a date; invite Ingrid Bergman (or, these days, let's say Olivia Newton-John or Robert Redford) to your variety show benefit. Imagine that anything is possible, and make a game of seeing how far you can go. The secret of the game is that we can go as far as God can go, and how far that is, is up to us to discover. There may be no way in the world you can do it — but there may be a way in God. Jesus said, *"In the world you shall have tribulation, but be of good cheer, for I have overcome the world."*

Success in life is purely a matter of *Intention*, a principal which very few people know how to make work for them. The Law of Intension is:

WE GET WHAT WE WANT.

Now you may answer, "Well, there are plenty of things that I want, but I haven't gotten them!" If, however, you are willing to examine your intentions clearly, you may discover that on some level there is a place in you that does not want it one hundred percent. Perhaps there is a part of you that is not sure if you really want it, or if you deserve it, or if you are ready for it. Or maybe there is something else you want more, and you feel you have to make a choice. Or perhaps you just don't believe it is possible. Whatever the reason for the roadblock, you and I are not victims of the fickle finger of fate. Each of us has meticulously chosen the story of our life. Our awakening to the reality of such responsibility is the dawn of making sense of turbulent experiences.

If we want to know what we really want in life, all we need to do is *look at what we are getting.* We can use our life as a mirror to see what our intentions actually are. Let's take an illustration. My friend Ron Young was in the process of producing his inspiring album *Love's Land,* when he ran short of funds. The record was nearly complete, but he needed several thousand dollars more to finish it, and the money was not coming. What to do?

Because Ron realized that what was happening "out there" was simply a reflection of a *spiritual* situation *within* himself, he decided to take an honest look at what was standing in the way of his album coming together. So he sat down and resolved to face the only person who could answer his question: *himself.* And what an important encounter it was!

"I realized that the album was not being completed because I had some doubts about it," Ron told me in his apartment late one evening. "In a strange sort of way, I was afraid to put myself out there, as if I could not see myself succeeding. It was something like facing my own self growing up, changing, coming into my own. Oddly enough, I had hesitations about it, as if staying the same was more comfortable, safer.

"Then I asked myself this question: 'Do I choose for this album to come out, or don't I? It has to be 100% 'Yes' or 100% 'No'; no in-betweens; no compromises; no mugwumps*. Either I go full force ahead on producing it, or I completely scrap it right now. What do I decide?'

"Then I decided it had to be '*Yes*' — It just had to. There could be no turning back because of fear or insecurity; I could not live my life in a childhood pattern just because it seemed safe. I had to go ahead. I had no idea where the money would come from, but I knew that if I declared my intention before God, it would come.

"The next morning when I went to work, one of my first clients asked me, 'Say, Ron, do you need any money for anything?'

" 'Funny you should ask! . . . My record needs a little more green energy to carry it over the hill. Why do you ask?'

" 'The other night I had a dream in which the numbers "1" and "7"

---

*mugwump: a person who sits with his mug on one side of the fence, and his wump on the other.

came to me very clearly. It was the kind of dream that was so real that I felt I had to do something about it. So this weekend I went to Atlantic City and played those numbers at the casino. Would you like to see what happened?'

" 'Sure would.'

"The man reached into his back pocket and took out his wallet, bulging at the seams. To my astonishment, he showed me twenty thousand dollars in cash! Then, right on the spot, he loaned me three thousand dollars at very low interest. *Love's Land* came out a few weeks later."

Ron's story presents us with the compelling teaching that he *attracted* that money to him by *affirming his intention* to complete that album. That completion came about only after Ron's decision was gelled within himself. Thoughts need thinkers to bring them to earth. Manifestation is in direct proportion to our concentration. God responds to "sort of" prayers with "sort of" answers. As one tongue-in-cheek philosopher put it, you can't be "sort of pregnant." Either you are, or you aren't. As Tom Wolfe coined the notion in *The Electric Kool-Aid Acid Test*, "You're either on the bus or you're off the bus." You're either on your way to your destination or you're standing on the corner. That's the point of Ron's story, this chapter, and the whole of life. The essential element of prayer and intention is *whole-heartedness*. If we pray or live half-heartedly, we will get half a result, which is the predicament in which most persons find their lives: half-here, and half-there. Such a way of living cannot lead to success, for as we are told in the Bible, "God spews the luke-warm out of his mouth." Hilda often says that it is better to be a whole something than a half-nothing. "Even if you're a rotter, kids, be the best rotter there ever was. If you go wrong, at least go wrong with a whole heart . . . Then when you come home to God, you will come home with a whole heart." Jesus gave the disciples the test of the parable of the two sons: "One said 'Yes' to his father and then did not do what he was asked; the other said 'No,' and later changed his mind and did his father's bidding. Which son did what his father wanted? The one who said 'No' and later turned about. This is why prostitutes and thieves were among Jesus' closest disciples. They were not luke-warm in their lives. They were whole-hearted in their sin, and when they discovered God, they were whole-hearted in their love for Him.

This brings us to the second leg of the Law of Intention:

**YOU DON'T HAVE TO KNOW HOW TO GET WHAT YOU WANT;
ALL YOU NEED TO KNOW IS *WHAT* YOU WANT.**

This is a subtle but paramountly important and exciting key to personal success. It means that there is much more to the universe than we have believed, and if we really expect to realize our dreams, we must allow God to deliver our blessings to us in ways deeper than we can plan or understand. There is an old saying that "The Lord moves in mysterious ways," and this is surely true. God is like the driver of a universal Greyhound bus. Once we have decided where we want to go, we can "sit back and leave the driving to Him." If we would just choose a nice window seat and relax, we would find ourselves at our destination in no time. Instead, we make it hard for ourselves because first of all we are not sure which bus to get on; we vascillate at the ticket counter, mulling indecisively over a number of possible destinations. The agent can't sell us a ticket if we don't tell him where we want to go. Then, once we've made our choice and we've stepped aboard the Greyhound to God, we immediately try to wrestle the wheel away from the Driver, insisting we know a better way. Then, even after we have surrendered the wheel and we arrive, we have a tendency to want to hide in the back of the bus, wondering if this is really where we want to go, and maybe we should turn back.

The good news is that we do not need to scheme and manipulate for our liberation. All we have to do is:

1. **Declare our intention,**
2. **Accept opportunities when they come,**
3. **Work with responsibility and confidence.**

We are all already liberated, and the game of life is a lesson in realizing that there is nothing we must do to be Divine. We just need to open up to the light within us. That is why Jesus said, "*Ask, and ye shall receive; seek, and ye shall find; knock, and it shall be opened unto you.*" Whenever I have tested the truth of these promises, they have proven themselves to be genuine. If you would like to prove them for yourself, I encourage you to ask — really ask — for something that you deeply want. Think of some aspiration that would change your life remarkably for the better: to heal a troubled relationship; to quit smoking; to understand something about yourself that you would really like to know; ask for anything that is important to you. Then find and underline these two verses in the Bible: "*Ask, and ye shall receive . . .*" and "*Thus saith God: Try me and prove me.*" Then hold God to His promise. Dare Him to prove that He can help you. Don't stop at the Pepsi Challenge — Go all the way. If God is really God, He has to come through. If He can't cut it, no one can. But He will. He has to. God wants so much for His Children to believe in Him that he seizes every opportunity to answer a prayer. God is like the owner of a great estate whose children don't come home because they have been deluded into thinking that their father is a pauper, or even that he is dead. Then, when he gets a collect call from one of his children who has gotten into deep trouble, and is so desperate that she is even willing to give her long-lost father a try for help, the father is overjoyed to do all he can to demonstrate his existence and his love. He will even fly out to the coast to bring his ailing child back to her rightful home. That's how happy and willing our Heavenly Father is to answer our prayers.

After we have contacted our Father, we must give Him time and space to do what He needs to do to answer those prayers. Sometimes it takes a while to get that flight to the coast. If we trust in Him, God will work out our help in just the right way, in just the right timing. It usually doesn't work to pressure God and try to force Him to answer a prayer by next Tuesday afternoon. If it really needs to be done by then, it will. If not, there is a reason, and we can afford to wait. If we feel frustrated about God's delay in answering a prayer, it is not a matter of God's ineptitude, but our impatience. If God is wise enough to know how to answer our requests, He certainly knows when they need to be answered. Jesus assured us, "*Your Father knows what you need before you even ask.*"

This perspective lifts prayer into a new light of personal promise. It means that we don't have to yell and scream at God to get Him to hear us. Because He lives in our very hearts, He hears our whispers as clearly as our shouts. He will respond more readily to one sincere thought than to a long but empty tirade. God appreciates quality over quantity. If He already knows what we need, we can simply sit peacefully and enjoy communing with Him. Perhaps the most powerful prayers are "*Thank you,*" "*I am,*" and "*I love you.*"

There is one footnote on the Law of Intention that must be recorded here: the element of *Grace*. This means that sometimes we don't get what we want, not because God can't deliver it, but because it is really not in our best interest to get it. As a priest once posed to me, "Does God answer *all* prayers? . . . Yes, He does," he explained, ". . . and sometimes the answer is 'No.' " This is not just an esoteric cop-out, but a very important principle to grasp, as it actually underscores the reality of the Law of Intention. It means that the level at which the request was made was not on a soul level, but on a desire or surface personality level, which is not congruent with the deep subconscious choice of the inner person, the soul. In other words, it is our *inner* self that actually decides (perhaps even before we were born) what we want and need in life, and the intention of the soul is so strong that little passing desires cannot supercede the soul's decision. For example, let's say that before you were born your soul (you) chose a life of service to humanity. Then when you get to high school you become influenced by rock music and for a few months you hope and pray to become an electrified superstar. So you write a schmaltzy fan letter to Jerry Garcia, pleading for a job as a roadie for the Grateful Dead. Then, when you don't get the job, you feel hurt and disappointed and you say, "The Law of Intention is not true . . . I asked for something and I didn't get it . . . There must be no God!" Then, let's say, the only job you can get is that of an assistant in a law office where you become fascinated by the possibilities for social change through community organizing. So you decide to go to law school, after which you find the most fulfilling experience of your life in serving as an advocate for the poor or the handicapped or the hungry. Then you look back on your fleeting desire to work for the Grateful Dead and you say, "Thank God I didn't end up doing that!"

I learned this lesson for myself in an experience that was not quite as glamorous as working for the Grateful Dead, but which was very important to me. When I was ready to go to graduate school, I applied to eight clinical psychology programs and one for counseling and guidance. I was rejected by nearly all of the clinical schools and accepted by the counseling program, at Montclair State College. For reasons which I could not explain, I felt so deeply drawn to Montclair that I didn't even bother to pursue the clinical route. Though I had no idea what was to come, it was through this program that I eventually met Hilda and my new spiritual life. Now I thank God that I did not get into those other schools, for now I realize that they were not really rejections, but *course corrections*, the universe steering me in the direction of the highest good for my soul's chosen evolution. So, you see, while I didn't get what my mind wanted, I did receive what my soul wanted — and that is the only result that really counts.

There is one more facet of the Law of Intention, an idea so powerful that it has changed my entire perspective on what life is about. It is a concept so exciting that I wish every human being could feel the thrill of it as I do, for it has truly made my life new. It is a secret of living which has been shouted and proclaimed throughout the ages, but yet remains largely untapped because only a handful of saints, sages, prophets, and free thinkers have realized its import and put it into action. This principle contains the power to make a pauper into a king, the downtrodden into the triumphant, and the crippled straight. It is nothing less than a gift from God to His Children, given freely to remove our miseries and make us alive again. It is the very key to heaven. I am speaking of the power of

BELIEF.

It is written in the scriptures, *"As a man thinketh in his heart, so shall it be."* Contained in this jewel of truth is the answer to making our lives what we want them to be. It means that we can literally create our experience with our thoughts and, because our minds are intrinsically unified with God's, we can make anything happen. That's a pretty potent assertion. I mean, it's not exactly what we've been told on television commercials which admonish us that we can't afford to leave home without our American Express card. The power of God is far greater than that of a credit card, and if we are willing to hold our beliefs up to spiritual light, we will find a golden treasure — perhaps the brightest — in these ancient prophetic words.

Let me offer a practical example. A friend of mine needed to discuss her HBO bill with the cable TV office. For weeks she tried to get them on the phone, but every time she called, the line was busy. She told me, "I just know they take their phone off the hook; someone told me that's what they do; I bet I'll never get them!" Somehow I could not believe that a public business would take their phone off the hook for weeks, so I asked her if I could give it a try. The phone rang three times, and someone answered . . . because I believed they would.

When we discussed why she hadn't gotten through, we discovered an even deeper reason: *She didn't really want to talk to them.* She had to challenge them on a dispute over her bill, and she didn't like having to do that. In other words, it was not her *intention* to make contact with them, and so she *created*, or attracted that line being busy every time she called. *"As a man thinketh, so shall it be."*

We need, then, to start thinking in new ways. We must believe we can get what we really want in life. We must, as one poet put it, "hitch our wagon to a star." As I figure it, God wouldn't plant any aspirations in our souls unless He was prepared to bring them to life. We are asked in the Bible, "Would God bring to the point of birth, and then not deliver?" In other words, would God impregnate our mind and heart with dreams of a better life that could not come true? I don't believe God would do that. I can't imagine Him finding any value in frustrating His Children. But I can imagine Him taking great delight in seeding a shining vision in our heart, and then watching us grow in strength until we align our life with His great intention for us, so completing our journey into Light.

No longer need we settle for table scraps or, like the prodigal son, the leftovers from the pigs' slop. We spend minutes, days, even lifetimes agonizing over petty hurts, measely pennies, and cheap ambitions, when we could be laughing in our Father's Kingdom. How much of my life have I underestimated the potential that the universe has imbued within me and my fellows! While God has been living in my very heart, I have searched and schemed after foolish desires. And now I, like you and the entire community of the spirit, am ready to come home. I am ready to claim my right to live as a light-filled being of free spirit. I joyously accept my part of an evolutionary step being made by millions of souls who are prepared to openly declare that love, truth, and goodness are the sacred elements of our life, and these blessings are to be known on earth as it is in Heaven. We are ready to affirm that God will take care of us without war, without nuclear power, without windfall profits, without separate drinking fountains for blacks and whites, without radiated food, without maiming animals to produce cosmetics. We are ready to live without fear and competition and alienation. We are ready to go for it. We are ready to support one another and to respect the earth and the air and the heavens. We are ready to acknowledge the holiness of all the blessed creatures that share the universe with us, and to honor their right to live and breathe as we do. We are ready to go for a New Age on the planet earth, a long-awaited era of harmony, good will, and the joy of mutual support. We are ready to recognize the oneness and the common aspirations of all peoples of all colors, ages, and sexes, and to celebrate the greatness of humankind's new destiny. We are ready to go for it now. We are ready.

Seeing and Believing

Paint a picture . . . hold to your vision
. . . and walk into your garden
— *Love's Land*, Ron Young

The doctor leaned back in his padded wooden chair and tossed his pen onto the blotter. "I'm afraid there's not much more we can do for your cancer, Mrs. Newhouse," he solemnly stated. "We'll continue with the chemotherapy and radiation treatment and just hope for the best." That night Mrs. Newhouse sat on her bed, frustrated and depressed. "What good is it?" she frowned. "Even the doctors don't have any hope!"

Then, as she sat in the quiet of that crucial night, a warm feeling began to well up inside of her, like a glowing ember that refused to be extinguished. It was a sense that there *was* something more that could be done, something greater than medicine, something bigger than chemicals and doctors and prognoses. But what?

Into her mind flashed the thought of her son, Jack, who she knew had been involved for years with what he called "holistic health." Jack had studied meditation, become a vegetarian, and taken up a number of spiritual practices that Mrs. Newhouse had dismissed as fads lingering from the 1960's. But now she felt an urge to ask her son more about what he was doing.

"I'm so glad you asked, Mom," replied Jack. "There's an excellent book that I think can really help you." Mrs. Newhouse jotted down the title of the book and immediately got into her car and drove to the bookstore, where she found *The Silva Mind Control Method* almost jumping off the shelf toward her. She eagerly plunged into the book, finishing it in just a few sittings, absorbing as much as she could. The principles of the book were simple: We create our lives, including health and illness, with our thoughts. To be successful and fulfilled, we must learn to use our minds constructively, using clear, positive images as building blocks. These mind pictures are absorbed into our sub-conscious, which in turn brings our new, uplifting thoughts into reality in the form of health, abundance, and peacefulness.

These principles seemed right to Mrs. Newhouse, somehow strangely familiar and comfortingly real. It was as if she already knew them, but had forgotten their truth. So Mrs. Newhouse began to practice the prescribed techniques. Every day for two sessions, one-half hour each, she would sit in a comfortable chair, relax, and visualize a bright light, something like a bolt of lightning flashing into the cancerous part of her body. Then she would visualize this light breaking up the cancerous cells, shattering them into thousands of tiny pieces. Again and again and again she practiced this picturing, until she saw her entire body as clear and whole and healthy.

Meanwhile, as the Law of Attraction would have it, Mrs. Newhouse was directed to another doctor who worked by the dynamic principles that she had discovered.

"It's very clear to me, Mrs. Newhouse," stated Dr. Holmes, "You can live and be healthy if that is what you choose. You must think positively and realize that there is a great Healer far more powerful than myself or any human being. If you attune your mind to this great healing energy, it will surely work for you."

This bright advice encouraged Mrs. Newhouse to continue even more enthusiastically with her visualization. Two weeks later she returned to the laboratory for x-rays. After completing the tests, the doctors walked out of the darkroom shaking their heads and checking the x-rays over and over and over again.

"We don't quite know how to explain this, Mrs. Newhouse," reported one of the medical team, "but your condition has improved considerably. As you can see on these x-rays, most of the cancerous cells have been broken apart, as if they have been *shattered*, and it looks like they are being expelled from your system!"

Mrs. Newhouse smiled and said a quiet prayer of thanks. Then she went home to visualize some more. Within a few months, Mrs. Newhouse was given a clean bill of health.*

---

*Hilda later explained that while the visualization was effective in this case, it is preferable to visualize only light and health, without giving any mental energy or reality to the negative situation, in this case, cancerous cells.

I would like to report a similar case which serves as an even more vivid demonstration of how the subconscious channels energy to create what it pictures. A young woman went to a healer for help for a condition of heavy acne. The healer picked up a magazine off a coffee table, thumbed through it, and carefully tore out a photograph of a glamorous model with a perfect "peaches and cream" complexion.

"Take this picture home and look at it for twenty minutes each day," prescribed the teacher. "Concentrate intently on it, as if you are looking in the mirror, and let the image of this lovely smooth skin be absorbed into your subconscious. You need to quit looking at your pimples and start appreciating your beauty!"

A week later the healer received another phone call from the young lady, now more distraught than before. "Something terrible has happened!" the girl exclaimed. "I must see you immediately!"

Within an hour the girl walked into the healer's apartment with a most unusual condition on her face. "Look!" she cried, "One side of my face has cleared up, but the other side still has pimples . . . I look even worse than before! How could this happen?!"

"Let me see that picture I gave you," requested the elder. As the girl took the photo out of her pocketbook, the answer became obvious: *The picture was a profile!* The girl had meditated on the image of one-half of a beautiful complexion, and because the subconscious absorbs and materializes exactly what it is given, half a clear complexion is exactly what she got.

To harness the great power of the creative subconscious mind to help us achieve our goals, we must understand how this magnificent, Divinely engineered machine works. It is a fascinating and marvelous tool, operating systematically on lawful principles, capable of making or breaking our life according to how we employ it. We can begin to take advantage of its treasures as we comprehend these basic ideas:

PRINCIPLES OF SUCCESSFUL LIVING

1. The life that God has given to us is entirely whole, complete, and perfect.

2. Our view of this perfect life depends on our thoughts, which filter reality into our perception of it.

3. If that filter is clear, like a clean, sharp lens, we experience and enjoy the perfection of life in its entirety.

4. If the filter is clogged by erroneous and negative thought patterns, the lens becomes distorted, and we see life as threatening, fearful, and bad.

5. This filtering takes place in the subconscious mind, below the level of our ordinary conscious awareness.

6. We can restore our vision of perfection by reprogramming the erroneous patterns and replacing them with positive, productive thoughts. The most direct and powerful way to accomplish this is:

VISUALIZATION	+	FEELING
Get a *clear mental picture* of what we want to be or accomplish,	then	*feel* as if it has *already* *come to pass.*

7. You and I can return to the perfect life that was intended for us through *positive thinking, seeing, feeling, speaking, and acting.*

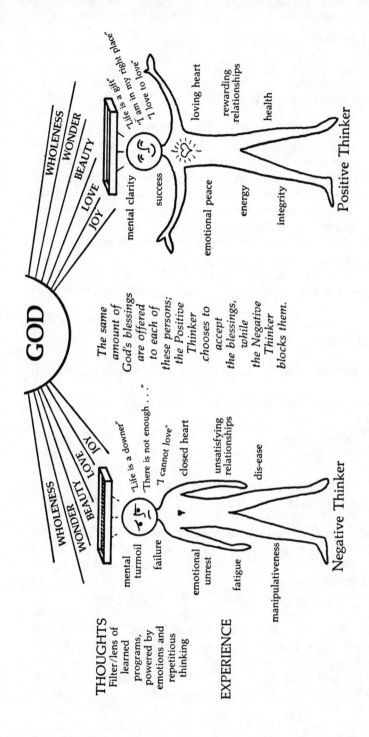

GOD

WHOLENESS
WONDER
BEAUTY
LOVE
JOY

"Life is a gift"
"I am in my right place"
"I love to love"

mental clarity
success

loving heart
rewarding relationships
health

emotional peace
energy
integrity

Positive Thinker

The same amount of God's blessings are offered to each of these persons; the Positive Thinker chooses to accept the blessings, while the Negative Thinker blocks them.

WHOLENESS
WONDER
BEAUTY
LOVE
JOY

"Life is a downer"
"There is not enough . . ."
"I cannot love"
closed heart

mental turmoil
failure

unsatisfying relationships
dis-ease

emotional unrest
fatigue

manipulativeness

Negative Thinker

THOUGHTS
Filter/lens of learned programs, powered by emotions and repetitious thinking

EXPERIENCE

HOW OUR THOUGHTS CREATE OUR EXPERIENCE
Abundant living is not a result of setting the world right, but *seeing* it *right.*

Let's look a little more deeply into the practical implications of these immensely important principles. As we can see from the story of the girl with acne, the subconscious is a powerful but *unbiased* computer that perfectly and literally carries out any program we feed into it, *even if the program is incorrect.* We have at our disposal an efficient, intelligently designed machine that will perform our every bidding, *even if we are unaware that the instructions it has received are not in our best interest.* This harsh but dynamic truth brings us to a crucial point: Because we human beings have free will and machines do not, it is *our responsibility* to *screen* and *critically evaluate* the programs we imbed in our creative mind, or else we must bear the brunt of faulty programming.

This eye-opening law was demonstrated to me by Susan Pitak, a hypnotherapist who received a complaint from one of her clients who had come to her to learn how to lose weight.

"I went home last week and practiced the methods you gave me," the lady reported, "but I ended up gaining ten pounds! What went wrong?!"

"Let's hear the relaxation suggestions you gave yourself," requested Susan.

"Well, I sat down, closed my eyes, and I began to tell my legs, 'You are getting heavier . . . and heavier . . . and heavier.' "

And so that is exactly what her legs got: heavier . . . and heavier . . . and heavier.

We have to be extremely careful of the words and pictures that we use; there is no such thing as an idle or meaningless expression. Because words contain the power of God ("*In the beginning was the Word, and the Word was with God*"), every thought we generate is registered in our subconscious which, as Dr. Eric Butterworth so aptly describes it, "cannot take a joke." In other words, even if we utter a phrase in jest or as a "figure of speech," the subconscious is busy recording what we say — simply because that is its job — and working toward materializing the idea it has "heard" us express.

This is the reason for the esoteric admonition to "*think and speak only those ideas which you want to see materialize.*" Conversely, this means that we do well to eliminate from our mental and oral vocabulary anything we do not want to see happen. Translated into practical terms, be careful to avoid phrases like, "If I have to go to that office one more time, I'll throw up!" or "I'm sick and tired of him!" unless you really want to throw up or be sick and tired. If you are not heedful of the thoughts and words you express, you might find that everyone else at the office is having a nice day and the person who you are sick and tired of is out playing tennis and having a jolly good time, while you may find yourself in bed — not because an office or person has any power over your health, but because you didn't realize that your subconscious mind heard your words as commands and quite readily responded by creating exactly the experience you described in your "idle" expressions.

Our problems are *not* caused by other people, poorly constructed bodies, or defective minds. They are caused by misunderstanding, lack of awareness, and misuse of the perfect tools that God gave us to work with. It is the poor craftsman who blames his tools for his errors. When we started out on earth — as individuals and as a human race — we had everything we needed to live in abundance, joy, and peace. There were no nuclear warheads, no polluted lakes, no lines on the earth that said, "That piece of land is yours and this one is mine." It was just a lovely garden. We got ourselves into trouble when we began to take what we had — especially the power to create with the mind — and use it incorrectly. Then, after we made a huge mess, we complained, "This world is rotten!" or "My mother made me neurotic!" or "There is so much suffering . . . There must not be a God!" But blaming is misdirected, wasted energy. We just need to realize that we processed a peaceful world through a subconscious belief system based on a fearful picture of life, and the results of that interpretation of God must be terrifying, for peacefulness is our nature, and any experience other than tranquility must, by virtue of who we are, leave us unsatisfied. We looked at the light of the world through dark lenses, and it is no wonder that we saw darkness. As the computer programmers label the problem, "G.I. — G.O." (*"Garbage In — Garbage Out"*). As the ancient seers labeled it: "G.I. — G.O." (*"God In — God Out"*).

I know a man whose experience of life is a cogent testimony to this law of mind. When he was a little child, Bob's father told him, "You'll be the death of me yet!" Then, when his father actually did pass on, Bob felt that he had caused his death, and he developed a stifling sense of guilt and unworthiness. This erroneous program hampered Bob's work and relationships for much of his life, until he found a positive spiritual group in which he learned to love himself once again.

Bob, like many of us, learned the hard way that many of the ideas we were taught as children are simply not true. For example: "Whites and blacks don't marry," or "You can't get anywhere without a college diploma," or "Men don't hug." Such false notions distort our view of life like a rock thrown into a calm pool disturbs the perfect reflection of the sky. We cannot really know God unless we learn to see life, love, and ourselves clearly. Seen through divine eyes, life, love, and ourselves are as we always have been: *perfect*. Only incorrect thinking can create problems where none exist.

Bob's story bears some very practical lessons. We have a paramount responsibility to scrutinize the beliefs about life that we were taught as children, and hold them up to the light of Truth. As children, we were very impressionable, without a mature ability to discern Truth for ourselves. As we have now grown into maturity, it becomes our responsibility to sift through what our childhood teachers told us, and *decide for ourselves* what is correct. We have no right to blame our parents or teachers for our unhappiness, for we now have free will to choose a path of life for ourselves and our world — an avenue of consciousness built upon the thoughts we *choose* to think. If we shirk the responsibility for discovering what is true, we have no one to hold accountable but ourselves, and no one will suffer for our erroneous programming more than ourselves. This may be a bold awakening, but Truth is not always gentle.

We also have an equally important (and perhaps even more crucial) responsibility to be *extremely* careful about the programs we offer our families, friends, and especially children. We must support our brothers and sisters with positive, encouraging, uplifting thoughts, and not pollute their consciousness with the brunt of limited thinking. One teacher pleaded that we never "crush a child's flower." This means that we must give one another every chance to succeed, to grow, to change for the better. If we mentally stifle another, we drag an aspiring soul into the mud of negation with us, and that's old fashioned bad karma. If you have ever had someone tell you, "You'll never do that," or "Forget it — You don't stand a chance of winning," or "Oh, come on — Be realistic," you can appreciate how important it is to uphold one another and give our family, friends, and co-workers every possibility to be great. Since we are all children of God, always learning and constantly needing nourishment to develop, the admonition to "give each others' flowers freedom to grow" applies to all of us.

This brings us to one of my favorite subjects, the consciousness of children. Jesus said that children are very close to God: *"If you want to enter the Kingdom of Heaven, you must become like a little child."* One of the wonders that I love about little children is the vividness of their imagination, their ability to see the magical and the exciting in all of life. The Sandman, Tooth Fairies, and Kermit the Frog are as real to children as mortgages and radial tires and governments are to adults. Through the eyes of a child, the world is ever fascinating, eternally new, and fully alive, and it is exactly this kind of vision that we must recapture if we are to re-enter the Garden of Eden, which is waiting for us in our very own heart.

One day I went to a fair with a little friend, Noah, and there we came upon "Officer Phil's Talking Car," an old VW Bug painted with a big happy smile and rolling eyes, glamorized with orange shag rug hair, and brought to life by a microphone through which Officer Phil (hiding behind the car) spoke to the fascinated children passing by. When the talking car asked my little Noah, "Is there anything you would like to tell me?" Noah shouted, "Yes! I love you very much!" which made Officer Phil about the happiest talking car at the fair.

It then occurred to me that it had been a while since I had told a car that I loved it, and it would probably make my life a little more joyous if I did occasionally tell a car — or a tree — or a typewriter — or a person, "I love you very much!" Noah's love for that car was as real as any that I have seen in most human relationships, maybe more so. Maybe that's why Noah, a silly kid who talks to cars, lives a lot of the time in the Kingdom of Heaven, and I spend quite a bit of my time in the state of New Jersey.

As Joni Mitchell so clearly puts it, "We've gotta get back to the garden." That garden is not to be found in the world as we have known it, but in *consciousness*: in our mind, in the way we look at life, in how much we are willing to let our hearts be free to accept the highest possibilities of who we are, what we are doing here, and what life is all about. As Jonathan Livingston Seagull discovered, we must allow our minds to soar above the flock. We must release our thoughts from the common petty burdens that bind men to insignificant details, and reawaken our visions of the grand and miraculous. We have to be able to see what we yearn to be — not who we were taught we are. We have to know there is much more to us — much, much more — than a name and a job description and a credit line and a difficult relationship.

We must remember that we are created in the image of God, the Source of the entire universe, and anything God can do, She can do through us.

That's the key. We need to quit asking God to fight through the mire of limited thinking, and allow Her to work *through* our positive minds. We can't walk around indulging in feeling bugged, creating turbulent storms of anger and depression, and then expect God to glide Her airplane of clarity through the hurricane and land on a muddy runway. We have to keep the runway clear. We don't have to be the pilot; if we just take care of the ground crew's job, the pilot will perform Her role. We don't have to create peace; I don't know any human being who can create such a Divine experience. All we need to do, as John and Yoko put it, is to "give peace a chance." That's all God wants — a chance. She just wants us to open the door of our heart a little bit — just a crack. Then She can let light into the room that we have sealed with many locks and shutters and then complained that God doesn't exist because we haven't been seeing light.

Jesus, the master psychologist, physician, and positive thinker, knew all of this, and this is how he taught it: "When you pray, you pray amiss! *Give thanks for the answers to your prayers before you receive them.*" In other words, we have to get the picture and the feeling of the health, success, or blessing that we want *before* we actually see it in physical form. There is a magnificent commentary on the story of the Jewish people crossing the Red Sea. It says that some of the Israelites went into the water *up to their necks* before the waters actually parted. That's faith. How could they walk in that far, unless they had a very clear vision that the waters would part? Their mind's eye had to be able to see that whole dry highway before their physical eyes saw one drop diminish. That's faith.

It seems to me that's the kind of faith, the quality of vision we need to make it through trying times. We need to know in our heart of hearts that even though the waters may be lapping up onto our shoulders, if we just stand firm on our vision of the rightness of life, of Truth, of God, the whole highway is already right here, and it won't be long before we're walking on solid ground. Actually, we have no choice but to have faith. What happens when we abandon right vision? The result is the world we have created around us, a terrifying nightmare of fear, divisiveness, and mistrust. Sometimes I think about what could be done with all the money and energy put into war, into false advertising, into competition. I think how the United States and the Soviet Union have each poured billions, perhaps trillions of dollars into a fictitious, fear-created "race for space" in which so many efforts have been unnecessarily duplicated and some of the greatest minds on the planet have been turned against each other instead of uniting in a common effort, because we believed in competition and not cooperation. Then I wonder how it all might be if someone, if enough someones, had a vision of humankind working together for mutual good, how much more practically could those trillions have been spent? Feeding hungry children. Delving into the scientific mysteries of life. Endowing the arts. Just thinking of the family of humankind nourished by harmonious cooperation is enough to keep me enthusiastic and eager and willing to work to build a new world.

Since I have discovered the miracle of thinking in alignment with high possibilities, I am keenly aware of how we use — and misuse — the power of our thoughts. While we could create unprecedented successes simply by believing in one another, too often we sadly deny ourselves the joy of mutual upliftment. Like atomic power, chemistry, and psychic abilities, all of which are gifts to celebrate the glory of life, we have taken the miracle of the creative power of thought and turned it against ourselves, dragging each other down instead of lifting each other up. I am very aware of the little signs and posters that secretaries and their bosses put up in offices. Before you tack up that plaque, please think about what you are creating, what kind of energy you are offering your brothers and sisters. In the front office of a big industry I saw this sign: "If something can go wrong, it will." I began to ponder on how that powerful thought filtered through the whole company. Every person who walked through those front doors, from the president to the visiting salesmen, had that program implanted in his or her subconscious and reinforced many times a day. One little sign. Then I began to imagine how much more money they might make, how much less illness they would experience, how much more joyous their jobs could be, if they had a sign like, "The universe is abundant," or "All things are working together for good!" or even "Welcome!"

Those were words. Let us consider pictures; their effect on the subconscious is even more powerful. (This is one of the reasons Jesus taught in parables; as the mind absorbs the picture images of the parables, they go directly into the subconscious through the right

91

hemisphere of the brain!) Perhaps you have seen the xeroxed cartoon of Snoopy going through the days of the week. The first day, Monday, he is happy, energetic, and dancing. Then follows a series of cartoons of Snoopy getting more and more tired and bedraggled as the days go by, until Friday, when he is laid out on the floor, completely exhausted. What do you think is the effect of that picture on the workers in that office, come Friday morning? No wonder burnout is such a big problem! When we post a sign or picture, we are feeding each other. I'm sure none of us would purposely give each other poison, so why would we mentally poison each other with thoughts of malfunction and tiredness? We just don't understand yet.

Around Halloween time one year I was passing by a hospital emergency room where I saw wall decorations of skeletons and ghosts and all kinds of horrible looking creatures. I began to wonder how this made the accident victims feel. I don't think it was very healing. Such errors in thought-expression are innocent enough, but their innocence cannot change the detrimental effects that such advertisements for negativity cost all of us. If we want to make positive strides for a healed world, we must realize the power of our thoughts and begin to use them toward the ends that we *consciously* choose. We must constantly be aware that every thought and picture that we express has the power of God behind it, and that is an extremely potent force with which we have been entrusted. So far, we haven't used it very well. But we can. All it takes is a moment of thought before we speak or act, just a few seconds to consider what we are creating with our words. More and more, I am trying to sieve my thoughts through my mind before I speak; I consider what the world would be like if the things I say were actually manifested. I am realizing that too often I have been prone to blurt out thoughts without considering their purpose or how they might affect the persons, world, and universe they touch. Now, as I am taking more moments to decide what I want to create, I am seeing more positive results coming from the words I choose. It's quite a profound lesson.

Once we realize that we can create better lives through right thinking, the purpose of living becomes clear and we begin to really make our thoughts and actions work *for* us. We come into our own; we make our time on earth useful, not only for each of us, but for all of us. That's when we start to put rainbow decals on the back windows of our cars, when we start to order bank checks with pictures of endangered animals in the background, and when we start to take down calendars with pictures of "The Great Disasters of the Twentieth Century" and replace them with photos of black and white children playing together. In one office I saw a quote by W. Somerset Maugham, a thought which I love: *"It's a funny thing about life, if you refuse to accept anything but the best you very often get it."* And I was so happy to see the bumper sticker, *"Miracles happen very day!"* That little sign literally blesses everyone whose eyes come to rest on it. I am grateful, too, to a friend who gave me a poster of the Sphinx with a great big Jewish star around its neck. The caption: *"Ya Gotta Believe."*

Yes, we've all gotta believe. There really is no choice about it now. The alternative is the world that we see out there, a horrible bedlam of war, hatred and incredibly painful human separation. The saddest part is not that it exists, but that *it is not necessary.* Suffering is not a painful fact of a random life, but the cumulative result of a long series of erroneous thoughts that began with the idea that "I am not enough." Every act of war is caused by someone who has lost the vision of his or her own beauty, who has traded in the sky of God for a roof in the suburbs, who has compromised his life's dream for a pension plan. If we are honest with ourselves, that is all of us, in some way. The wars in Vietnam and the Falklands are not caused by unenlightened presidents and juntas; they are the tip of the iceberg of consciousness, the greater part of which lies below the surface, a chunk which is shared by everyone on the planet. That's me and you. It's a heavy one to own, but we can no longer afford to make the bad guys "out there." There's something of a hawk in all of us, and we have to admit to it before we can reconcile it. I'm not saying we are bad guys; quite to the contrary. God knows we are beings of the holiest light, His very children, to be sure. We just forgot who we were, and we settled for skeletons on the wall of the waiting room instead of flowers. As soon as we see that it is *we* who have posted the skeletons, we realize that it is *we* who can take them down and replace them with the light of the saints. The last — and only — trick of the devil (unconsciousness) is to try to get us to think that we are powerless prisoners of a heartless world, thrown into a whirlpool of confusion by a whimsical and sadistic fate. I say that we are born of the highest and only Goodness of the universe, and our beauty is incomparable in all of creation, because that splendor is the very Light of God shining through us, imbued by the Creator Himself.

The men I most admire are visionaries. There is something about the word "visionary" that awakens a deep thrill within me and makes my soul resonate with inspired strength. If I am to be anything in this life, I want to be a visionary. I want to be able to see beyond what now presents itself as real. I want to look past appearances and recognize what can be. I want to be able to dream and let my mind soar free, unbound by the chains that shackle most peoples' thoughts to little things. I want to know that God would not show me anything that is not possible, that everything I can imagine I can become. I want to know that there is a Living Force of the whole of the universe that enfolds me simply because I live and breathe. I must see. I must believe. I must be a visionary. I cannot be anything else.

What God Can Do

All things are possible to him who believes.
— Jesus the Christ

It was a rainy night in Louisiana, and it seemed as if there was nothing the rescue crew could do. A young man in a new sports car had skidded off the road and wrapped the shiny machine around a tree, trapping him behind the wheel. As he cried out for help, the squad worked feverishly to unjam the mangled door. Crow bars, blow torches, and pulleys had failed. What now?

It was just then that a frail black man was walking by the scene of the accident. "What's happened?" he asked.

"The boy is stuck in there," a somber voice returned. "We're waiting for more equipment, but he's hurt and time is running out."

Without further discussion, the small man pushed his way through the crowd around the car, placed his hand on the jammed door's handle, took a deep breath, and pulled the door open. Immediately the rescue crew dashed to the driver and helped him crawl out of the wreck. Then they turned their attention to look for this unlikely superman who had done what power tools could not, but he was nowhere to be found.

Word of this miraculous deed spread along with a search for the hero. Several days later his identity was discovered: he was an illiterate hired hand on a local poultry farm. A reporter from the city newspaper was dispatched for an interview.

"How did you do it?" the reporter queried.

"Oh, you'd be amazed what God can do when He needs to get something done!"

What God can do. God can do anything. He can give us the strength to open mangled car doors. He can resolve troubled relationships. He can change a life of pain and sorrow into a testimony of joy and triumph. What God can do.

95

I would like to share with you some of the wonderful things that I have seen God do. I have, for example, seen Him fill teeth and change silver fillings to gold. This may sound like an unusual kind of miracle for God to perform, but there is no challenge too small for God's loving attention. If God knows "every hair on our head," as it says in the Bible, He must surely know every tooth in our mouth! And if He can make the crippled walk, He must certainly be able to straighten teeth. I had the good fortune to attend a healing service by Rev. Willard Fuller, a dynamic and powerfully faithful minister through whom God works the wonder of healing teeth. Rev. Fuller's healing services have had over thirty thousand persons report dental healings, from silver fillings changing to gold, to root canal work being accomplished instantly, to a whole new set of teeth growing in to the mouth of a person who had worn dentures for many years.

As I sat in the audience of Rev. Fuller's service, I heard him tell his inspiring story: Many years ago he was in great pain, diagnosed as having incurable rheumatoid arthritis, which the doctors said would become "only more painful." But Rev. Fuller was not about to accept this fate. He remembered reading in the Bible, *"This kind cometh out but by fasting and prayer."* So he fasted and prayed, and several days later he was healed — just like that. In a moment, he felt the pain leave him and he got up and walked, free of arthritis. "And since that moment," tells Rev. Fuller, "I have not had one bit of discomfort from a disease that was supposed to cripple me."

Several years later Rev. Fuller met another healer, Rev. McCabe, who prophecied that he would be given the gift of healing teeth — and that is exactly what happened. I remember so clearly the vibrant moment when Rev. Fuller shared his living faith with us: "I believe God can do *anything!* . . . I know He can . . . I *know* it! . . . I *know* it! . . . I know for *sure* that He can heal teeth . . . I've seen Him heal thousands of dental problems before my eyes!"

And I saw it, too. During the service a friend of mine looked into

Rev. and Margaret Fuller can be contacted to arrange a healing service, or for personal prayer, at this address:
The Lively Stones World Healing Fellowship
P.O. Box 2007
Palatka, Florida 32077

her mouth with a mirror, and every one of her porcelain fillings had turned to bright, gleaming gold. I saw this for myself. The gold was so shiny that I could see it glistening from across the room. As more and more persons examined their teeth, I saw their eyes bulge to find gold fillings where there had been silver ones, straight teeth where they had been crooked, and comfort where there had been pain. What God can do.

This demonstration opened my mind to the exciting possibility that there *is* a bigger reality — another dimension of life — than the one in which I was living. That night it became clear to me that if God can fill teeth, *He can do anything*. Please realize with me what this means: it means that there is *no disease* that is incurable. Every disease that there has ever been — including cancer, brain damage, and leprosy — has been cured. If there has ever been one person who has been cured of cancer, that means that *cancer is curable,* and anyone who says it is not, or gives odds on someone's chances of recovery, is simply not telling the truth. *Healing is completely up to God and the individual soul* (which are One), and even the best clairvoyant cannot say for sure who can be healed and who cannot. As Shakespeare's Hamlet said, "There are more things in heaven and earth than are dreamed of in your philosophy, Horatio!"

Anything is possible. I have had the privilege to witness healings which can only be described as miracles of God. At Hilda's meetings I have seen persons healed of glaucoma, cancer, and multiple sclerosis. I have seen Rev. W.V. Grant of Cincinnati receive a woman who had been deaf for many years, pray for her in the name of Jesus Christ, and instantly she could hear. Padre Pio, a holy man in Italy, prayed for a man who had *no cornea*, and sight was restored to him. If God can give sight where there is no cornea, there *must* be a *power in the universe greater than the flesh.*

Jesus knew the reality of such a power, and it was through this awareness that he was able to raise Lazarus from the dead. When he approached the tomb, Jesus did not say, "It's too bad about Lazarus," or "Maybe God might hear our prayers for Lazarus," or "I hope Lazarus can be raised." He did say, *"Lazarus: Come forth!"* — and out walked Lazarus, renewed. Jesus *knew* there is a higher dimension of life than disease, dead bodies, and weeping sisters. He understood that eternal life is real and death an imposter, and this was the knowledge that gave him the authority to command a dead man to walk out of the tomb.

It was this very same truth that inspired St. Paul to teach,

BE RENEWED BY THE RENEWING OF *THE MIND*.

We want to be renewed and energized, but too often we seek to renew our soul, which is *spiritual*, with things and experiences which are physical. We have tried drugs, money, sex, power, relationship after relationship, travelling to exotic countries, and worshipping heroes (at least those are the things I have tried), but after the initial wave of each new excitement dissolves, we find ourselves somehow a little more empty than before, a little more hollow, a little more frustrated. This is because we are attempting to satisfy *spiritual* hunger with *physical* experience, and because we are *spiritual beings* — akin to angels — we cannot be satisfied by earth experiences. *Spirit can be satisfied only by spirit*. Mind cannot be completed by matter — only by the renewing of: *the mind*.

We are like voyagers who have travelled for aeons over rocky hills and through green hamlets, up sharp crags and down gentle streams, braving our way through the bleakest winters and savoring the mildest springs. We have known the joys and sorrows of life in so many different ways on this fantastic adventure of awakening. Now our long journey through experience has brought us to a crucial point. We are realizing that our attempts to find lasting peace through physical experience have not borne the fulfillment we expected. Our efforts to know God through the body have brought us momentary flashes of pleasure, but in the long run they have left us unsatisfied. To some, life seems to be a cruel series of disappointments.

From the soul's point of view, however, these frustrations have actually served as blessings, each one pointing us inward, bringing us closer to our real identity, our Home in the Spirit. Verily we stand now at the threshold of a kingdom of riches and splendor that far outshines any gold our eyes have beheld. *"The Kingdom of Heaven"* that we sought in the outer world *"is within,"* and we can freely enter into it by the turn of one simple key: *the mind*.

This critically important mind has a dual potential: it can serve as a healer or act as a merciless slayer, depending on how we use it. The mind is like a switch that controls the lights in a temple. In the right position, the switch completes the circuit and the light reveals masterpieces of inspired expression that lift us into the sacred simply by our beholding them. Switched off, however, the circuit is incomplete, and the wonders of the temple are lost in darkness, invisible to those who long to be blessed by them.

Rev. Fuller gave an example of how the mind can shut the light out from where we need it most. A little girl came to him after having a great deal of dental work. Rev. Fuller prayed, and every single cavity and filling in the girl's mouth disappeared, leaving a mouthful of perfectly clean, white, whole, cavity-free teeth. When the girl's happy parents took her to the dentist to show him what God had done, the dentist did not believe them. After pacing back and forth many times, examining and re-examining her mouth and her x-rays and consulting with the dental assistants, he angrily accused them, "You have switched daughters on me!"

It is but our thoughts that determine whether we enter laughing into the Kingdom of Heaven, or stand weeping at the gate. If our mind is cluttered with narrow "one-way-to-do-it" beliefs, we cut ourselves off from the help that could make our path through life so much clearer and easier. If, however, we are open to new ideas, bigger possibilities, and outright miracles, we literally invite God and all of His blessings into our life.

This is why Jesus, Hilda, Rev. Fuller, and all other spiritual masters have told us that if we want to enter the Kingdom of Heaven, we need to quit thinking so much. My favorite movies these days are Walt Disney family-type triple G movies. I used to think they were just corny, unsophisticated, silly stuff, but now I revere them as delightful sunbeams. There is a scene in *E.T.* in which the neighborhood boys, attempting to save E.T., are being pursued from all sides by marching battalions of police and F.B.I. men. Just as it seems the boys are hopelessly trapped, suddenly they and their bicycles are lifted off the ground (by E.T.'s faith), and they fly over the hills to E.T.'s safe homecoming. (When we run from our problems on the level at which they can attack us, we are quite at their mercy. But when we allow Faith to lift us above them and we look at them from an innocent perspective, God somehow finds a way that we haven't thought of, one which will save us in a way that we could not save ourselves.)

When I saw those kids begin to fly on their bicycles, tears of joy welled up in my eyes. There was something so uplifting and free, even holy, about allowing that to happen. It was as if I remembered a lost magical realm that I knew and loved in my childhood, a sunlit land in which everything was real. That scene made me remember giggling as Peter Pan took Wendy by the hand and guided her to Never-Never Land, and cheering for the Lone Ranger when he survived the ambush by the Butch Cavendish Gang, and feeling so excited when Little Lulu met the spacemen at her bedroom window. I was transported to a childhood realm where anything could happen, where everything was alive and dancing and in harmonious relationship with everything else. As I look back now, I see that for me life ceased to be fun when I stopped believing that anything could happen, and it became exciting again when I began to believe in miracles.

That's the secret: believing in miracles. We always have to be open to the possibility that something wonderful can happen — something that we haven't thought or dreamed of — something that can really get us out of the mess we seem to be in. We have to know 100% that there is always a way out, even if we haven't discovered it yet. Dr. Robert Mueller, Assistant Secretary General of the United Nations, tells how he was cornered by the Nazis in a French hotel. Hiding in an attic, trying to figure out how to escape, he thought, "This is my moment of opportunity!" At that moment an idea flashed to him: he took off his glasses, parted his hair the opposite way, walked down into the lobby, right into the crowd of Nazis searching for him, and he asked, "What's the commotion here?" "Have you seen a Mr. Mueller?" asked one of the guards. "Yes," he replied, "he was just upstairs." Immediately the soldiers charged upstairs and Mr. Mueller walked out the front door, free.

It's that flashing, that moment of inspiration, that wafting of an insightful thought from a realm higher than the $2+2=4$ reality — that's what God can do. It is rare that we reason out the solution to our problems. More often our answers come in an intuitional awakening, an "Aha!" moment for which we cannot really take credit or say, "This was *my* thought." At best, we can say, "This thought was given to me." Albert Einstein, who had one of the greatest thinking minds in human history, said, *"I have not arrived at my understanding of the universe through the rational mind."*

There is a poetic verse from a lovely song by Sue Daniels: *"Open up your heart . . . Tear it all apart."* When I first heard these lyrics, they seemed to be a little contradictory. I mean, opening up your heart is so sweet, and tearing it all apart seems so coarse, so heavy. After listening to the song several times, however, I began to understand what it means. In order for our hearts to really be open, we must tear up all the old, limited, tight beliefs that we held about who we are and what life is. These are thoughts that once served us at a stage of our awakening, but there comes a time when they have outlived their usefulness. After a certain point they only bind us, and we must make space for a new, more glorious reality to take their place. We cannot live in a consciousness of God and limitation at the same time: "No one can serve two masters," said Jesus. There are either miracles or death, no in-between. Either Lazarus is dead for good, or there is God. That's what it comes down to.

I would like to conclude these thoughts by sharing with you an extremely powerful affirmation which has worked miracles in my life. I offer it to you with the confidence that it can work as wonderfully for you, should you choose to use it. It is this:

GOD CAN DO ANYTHING.

Read this affirmation out loud now, several times, emphasizing a different word each time. Then repeat it to yourself mentally, over and over, concentrating and contemplating the truth of the idea, until you realize that this affirmation was written especially for you, right now, given as a perfect answer for this particular moment of choice in your life, a life that is very important to God. Then, after the truth of the affirmation is blazing in your heart, think of several situations in your life that may be troubling you. One by one, hold each situation up to the light of the affirmation, and repeat the affirmation as if it applies particularly to that problem, until the light of the truth of the affirmation makes the problem evaporate like mist before morning sunlight. Then, during the course of your day, if any trouble assails you, bring forth the affirmation into your mind, and realize that these words are absolutely, eternally, and unalterably true. They are words of God.

Repeating this affirmation literally rearranges our atoms and aligns every cell of our being with the Almighty Power of the Living God. Moreover, it attunes and connects us with the strength of Jesus Christ, Moses, Buddha, Mohammed, Lao Tse, and every great soul, saint, and prophet that has ever demonstrated the victory of the spirit over limitation. Because these words are true, they have the power to lift us up

101

on a wave of momentum that immediately disintegrates all negative thought patterns and delivers us into a new life that will stand as a living testimony to the truth that God is real, He is the only power in the universe, and He lives in you as you. Realizing this truth sets into motion a snowball of awakening that shines onto and is magnified by every person you and I touch with our faith in our mutual Divinity. It renews our joy and allows us to be children again. It answers all of our prayers and heals our broken dreams to reveal that they were never anything less than whole. It shows us a dynamic vision of who we truly are, and how important we are to God in His plan to give loving birth to a new and better world. It makes us complete, free, and literally Divine. That's what God can do.

What Goes Around

And in the end, the love you take
is equal to the love you make.
— The Beatles

As my friends and I approached the toll booth at the George Washington Bridge, an unusual and intriguing idea flashed to me: Let's pay the toll for the car behind us! It would be the kind of thing that would make someone's day just a little nicer, a rare kind of touching, impossible for the most cynical commuter to ascribe an ulterior motive, and a gracenote on the highway of human relations that would make life on earth a bit more fascinating for everyone involved. So each of us contributed fifty cents, smiled to the toll collector, and we watched him quizzically wrinkle his brow as we passed. That was about five years ago.

Several months ago I was returning to New Jersey from Pennsylvania via the Dingman's Ferry Bridge, a quaint old country crossing that I love to travel, just to hear the creaks of the old wooden planks under the wheels. As I pulled up to the toll booth of this tiny antiquated span, I readied my money for the attendant, an amiable elderly fellow who gives everyone a treat of country conversation with their change.

"No, thank you," he twinkled at me, "that won't be necessary . . . The fella in the car in front of you just paid your toll . . . Just go right on ahead!"

I put my change back in my jacket pocket, nodded "thank you" to the kindly attendant, and chuckled as I stepped on the accelerator. Then, as I passed the toll station, I noticed the sign posting the amount of the toll: *fifty cents.*

What goes around, comes around. What we send out into the universe is returned to us in appropriate nature and equal measure, by a Law and a Mind far greater and more exact than any mortal

103

calculation can fathom. Jesus said it this way: "Cast your bread on the water, and it shall return to you." He told, too, that "The Father knows every sparrow and every hair on your head," — and every fifty cents you give at a toll booth.

In the Eastern tradition it has been called *karma: As ye sow, so shall ye reap.* It is a principle basic to every religion and system of cultural ethics, given by God in different words and languages at different times to reach all people. But no teaching of karma is as clear as direct experience.

I had such an experience with my friend Danny Holaday, who for many years owned a local health food store called *Nature's Kitchen.* Danny is one of the most loving and giving persons I have ever known; he is extremely generous in allowing his store to be used for classes and community activities, at no charge. I remember, too, when I approached Danny about selling some books, he gave me a better deal than I asked for. He simply loves to give. Unfortunately, being a nice guy does not always seem to coincide with running a business (at least that's what we have been taught), and over the years while Dan was making so many people happy, the store was running into debt. The Holadays came to the point where they just didn't know how they were going to meet the next month's bills — but Danny wasn't worried.

Then one day all that had gone around, came around. A man in a three-piece suit walked into the store and asked to speak to the manager. Danny invited him into the office and the well-dressed man began to speak:

"Mr. Holaday, I represent a large vitamin company which is about to market a new line of vitamins which we plan to distribute on a national level. We would very much like to use the name "Nature's Kitchen" for our line, but we find that you have registered this as the name of your store. We would like to obtain the rights to use that name, and we are prepared to pay for it . . . Would twenty thousand dollars be suitable?"

Of course it would. Now the company's vitamins are called *"Nature's Kitchen,"* Danny's store is (most appropriately) renamed *"Nature's Holaday,"* and what went around has come around. It works.

Over the years, *karma* has gotten a bad name, bad press. How often I have heard or thought, "You better not do that . . . it's *BAD*

KARMA!" or "This must be my *BAD KARMA* coming back on me!" and so on. There is, to be sure, great wisdom in the need to give forethought to our acts, and to see how we actually bring difficulty upon ourselves. But somehow, when I hear the way the word *karma* is often used, it seems that it should be accompanied by a dramatic, ominous vibrato on the bass notes of an old player piano, as if Mr. Poison Zumack (the caped, black-hatted, curly-waxed-moustached villain on the old *Rootie Kazootie* show, who was always trying to steal Miss Polka Dottie's polka dots) is about to jump out from behind a curtain, snarling a sinister laugh, with the overdue mortgage in hand. But I don't think it is really that way; I don't believe any karma is completely bad.

We need to look at karma in a positive light to really see how this magnificent, God-ordained principle actually works *for* us. We need to look into the laws of sowing and reaping, from a high, masterful, *appreciative* perspective. We need to open to the truth that when our "bad" karma comes back to us, it is a gift from God, generously and graciously allowing us to learn how we have strayed from Her loving arms — and showing us, too, the way to return.

Some obvious examples of the way that "bad" karma is actually very helpful are physical illness, relationships, and work. I met a very calm and easy-going man who told me, to my surprise, that he had recovered from a heart attack. "You seem so tranquil now," I noted. "Yes, I am," he agreed, ". . . but if you had known me five years ago you would have seen a nervous wreck. I felt tremendously uptight and driven . . . You might say I was overworking at the expense of my peace. Then, when my heart gave me a very clear message about the way I was approaching life, I realized I had to make a choice: Cool out or die. I decided to make a major change in the way I was living my life, and the person you are looking at now is the result of that change. I'm about a hundred times happier now."

The same principle holds true for the area of relationships. When we are in close relationship with another person, we learn where we are holding out on the universe, and where we need to let go. If we are attached or clinging in any way, the tension that we feel must eventually yield to the realization that it feels a lot better to give love than to make demands, and somehow we learn to release the other person. The miracle is that as soon as we free our partner, we free *ourself.* Jealousy is a good example of this way of growth. In one of my relationships, I felt jealous to the extent that it jammed the signal of the love that was flowing between us. At some point I realized that the times in our relationship when I didn't feel jealous were much more rewarding than the moments I made demands, and I really wanted to become more flexible. As I eased up, my enjoyment of the flow of love increased so much that I knew I had hit upon the right way to do it. The process of growth was not easy and it was not smooth, but it was something I had to go through to become free. Now I honor that difficult but necessary lesson as a gift.

Similarly, when we go out to earn a living, we have got to get it together. I think that the most embarrassing moment of my life was when I fibbed my way into a job as a waiter at a shore hotel. I wanted to earn some quick money, so I applied for work for a busy holiday weekend, and I told the maitre d' that I had experience — which I didn't. When Saturday morning breakfast came early and busy, and twenty people filed into my station, I was faced with the stark and unenviable realization that I didn't know what half of the foods in the kitchen were, and these people, who had paid a handsome rate for the weekend, wanted exotic variations on their eggs that I couldn't even pronounce. I mean, I didn't even know the difference between oatmeal and farina. All I remember is running back and forth from the dining room to the kitchen, pleading with other waiters for help, and wishing I could just pinch myself with the pickle tongs and wake up. The highlight (or lowlight) of the debacle was when one woman who had been sitting and waiting and waiting and waiting for her order (which I kept forgetting), began to weep and plead, "Please . . . just bring me *something* to eat . . . I don't care what it is . . . I'll take anything!" I think some people thought they were on Candid Camera (and if I was smart, I would have told them they were). But I was too embarrassed to think of anything clever like that. All I could think of was the invisible man, who suddenly became my ideal. I would have dived right into the farina (if I had known what it was).

Those three breakfast hours were perhaps the longest of my life, and they were also one of the most ruthlessly compassionate lessons that my Heavenly Father has ever shown me. That was the last time I ever lied about my experience. Even if for no other reason than to avoid extreme embarrassment, I had to get my act together. So the bad karma turned out, in the long run, to be very good indeed.

It seems to me that the only predicament worse than "bad" karma would be *no* karma, or no system of feedback by which we could learn. This would be like a thermostat that doesn't register when the temperature drops to the point where the heat needs to go on, or a sprinkler system that doesn't activate when smoke touches its sensor. We may feel that pain is a bad thing, but how cruel would God be if we were allowed to put our finger in a fire without some kind of warning that it would damage our body? Or if we were able to over-draw our checking account without limit, without notice, and then later be required to pay it back in full? Or if we were allowed to head toward destroying our earth with radiation, without a Three-Mile-Island malfunction to wake us up? To me, all of these possibilities seem more cruel and unthinkable than the notion that there must be no God because there is pain in the world. To the contrary, there must be a God who cares enough to teach us.

But in order for the Grace of that teaching to be complete, we must be *teachable*. We must open our minds to the possibility that the universe is bigger than the narrow, contracted world we once believed in. Some may say that "karma" is unscientific, but as I see it, karma is the absolute essence of all science: every act has a predictable effect. The ideas that we plant in our minds magnify themselves in our lives, and we create our own reality by the situations to which we give our attention. This was taught to me by Diane, who watched one soap opera so much that when one of the characters in the plot died, several of Diane's friends sent Diane sympathy cards! Or consider those who win the lottery. (Besides the fact that such people were probably philan-thropists in previous lives), it is clear that those who win had to set the wheels in motion by buying a ticket. That's cause and effect. And then there is the case of Duane Alster, who was the head of the yippies in my town when they gave the police such a hard time at campus demonstrations in the late '60s. What is Duane doing now? He is a police officer in the same town, having to deal with kids like he used to be. Duane cast his stone into the lake years ago, and now he must ride the ripples of the waves he created.

This masterfully engineered system, perfect right down to soap operas and lottery tickets, is designed specifically for our awakening, our renaissance into higher consciousness, the peace which every soul seeks. This is why Hilda sometimes tells persons who have been hurt, "You ought to be glad that you paid off a bit of your karma; now you're that much closer to Freedom!" This wondrous life teaches us in two ways: the "good" karma rewards us and gives us a clue that we are on the right path home, and the "bad" karma wakes us up, shakes us out of a nightmare. Though we may sleep in private houses with locked doors, we live in an inescapably public universe in which we must all eventually realize that our being here is not a fruitless treadmill on a trip to nowhere, but a living, breathing heartbeat in the great body of God, intrinsically connected with every other spark of life that has ever or will ever live.

This awesomely empowering lesson of our potential clicked with me one morning when I was studying an orange seed. It occurred to me that within this tiny seed there was a whole orange tree, and hundreds more, and perhaps millions more. Within this one little seed, the size of a speck, lay the potential for feeding hundreds or thousands of people. Then it occurred to me that only oranges could come from this seed — no apples, no bananas, no grapefruits — only oranges. This insight gave me tremendous encouragement to take care in the thoughts and acts that I plant in the universe. It gave me hope and enthusiasm that the positive works I generate can bear fruit and really have an impact on the world — that my ideas do *not* exist in a vacuum, and that what I do in this life really does matter: *If this little orange seed could feed thousands of people, what then is the potential of one loving word?*

Then an even broader and more stunning thought occurred to me: Whenever I or you do an unkind, unthinking, or hurtful act, it is simply because we do not realize that our acts count, that there is a greater, grander system of the cosmos than our meager day-to-day affairs. This thought made me a little sad, for it said to me that many of the people in the world are in despair about the importance of their lives, about God, about their ability to have a meaningful effect on the lives of those they touch. Then I understood that violent acts can come only from persons who are feeling small, unloved, and powerless. With this realization a great wave of compassion flowed into my heart, for in that moment I saw that all of the wars, all of man's inhumanity to man, and all of the aloneness in our world is born of good, godly beings who don't realize who they are. Warmakers are simply children of God, grown to physical maturity and a social position where their decisions affect many people, but who are still scared children inside. They have lost the awareness and faith that we are all known, important, and cherished by our Heavenly Father. The irony of men making war is that it is always in search of peace. It is only when one does not know inner peace that he or she seeks it in the outer world.

Our quest for peace is fulfilled as we recognize the amount of love God has invested in our well-being. The great teaching of karma is that no matter what we have done or how far we have strayed from the path, God keeps on loving us and guiding us home like the great beam of a lighthouse on a stormy, rocky shore. He is willing to put up with our zany stubbornness and set us afloat no matter how many times we start to sink because we think we have to rock the boat (when all we need to do is set our sails in the right direction). I tell you, God must have the patience of a saint. Perhaps He sees something in us, something very good — even Divine — that makes His corrections worth His while. Perhaps, as Jesus saw the fishermen as fishers of men, God is aware of the eternal Light within us, a shining goodness that we have not acknowledged because we have been mesmerized by the throbbing disco-lights of the world. He is willing to stick it out with us until we grow out of our silly belief that we are abandoned offshoots of accidental evolution, and into the great memory that we are Sons and Daughters of a living God. In His infinite compassion, our Father is willing to communicate with us on any terms we accept. If we are a little too caught up in life to hear His gentle whispering, He speaks to us through the grosser lessons of earth experience, giving us a report card on our progress on planet/school earth, with a little love note telling us that no matter how many times we fail, we can try again until He has the proud pleasure to shake our hand on graduation day. That's the day we realize that all of the smiles and helping hands that are extended to us are ones that we have previously given, like ripples in a universal lake, returned to us years (perhaps lifetimes) later, with the perfect loving exactness of a fifty-cent toll.

Coming Home

New Possibilities for Loving

A human being is a part of the whole, called by us "Universe," a part limited in time and space. He experiences himself, his thoughts and feelings as something separated from the rest — a kind of optical delusion of his consciousness. This delusion is a kind of prison for us, restricting us to our personal desires and to affection for a few persons nearest to us. Our task must be to free ourselves from this prison by widening our circle of compassion to embrace all living creatures and the whole nature in its beauty.

— Albert Einstein

One evening Hilda asked a group of us, "Kids, what did you come to earth for?" Feeling that I had the right answer, I rose and said, "Love."

"Oh, isn't that sweet!" Hilda replied in the kind of sing-song tone of voice that hinted that I was about to be taught a lesson.

"Let me ask you this, then," Hilda continued, "Is there anyone that you love more than anyone else?"

I didn't have to think long before I answered, "Yes."

"Then you haven't lived up to your potential yet, for your work is not complete until you experience the joy of loving all as you love the one you love the most."

I turned to *The Messiah's Handbook*, a journal of wisdom revealed to Richard Bach by Donald Shimoda in his *Illusions: The Adventures of a Reluctant Messiah.** There I found: "*Here is a test to find whether your mission on earth is finished: If you're alive, it isn't.*"

I have thought for years about Hilda's lesson, highlighted by the words of the Reluctant Messiah, trying hard to understand what she was teaching me. Her instruction about loving seemed to challenge so

---

Illusions: The Adventures of a Reluctant Messiah, Dell Publishing Co., Inc., 1977.

many of the ideals I had held for so long, beliefs about romance, about specialness, about family, about life. This love that she spoke of seemed so new to me, yet strangely familiar and satisfyingly real. Such an idea of loving forced me to look deeply into myself to try to discover what love is and what it means to truly love someone. How many times I have said, "I love you," and how many times, I wondered, have I really felt the reverence those sacred words deserve? Had I been a hypocrite, cheating the Truth from my brothers and sisters by speaking words I only half-understood? Or did the words "I love you" bear a blessing even if I was not conscious of their real meaning? I had to know what love is. I had to know why God gave us the ability to love. I had to take love by the hand and with it approach the altar of Truth and submit both of our beings to the Light of God, with the demand to know what we were created to be.

The answer I was shown was at first frightening, then unsettling, and ultimately liberating. I saw that Hilda and Donald Shimoda were correct. I had created distinctions between who I could love and who I could not, divisions as artificial as the lines on a map, borders that exist only in the mind of man, separations which the exultation of nature does not recognize. I saw that I had manufactured notions of who is lovable and who is not. I had treated love — a spirit — like a commodity by reserving it for certain persons — those who loved me — and withholding it from the rest. I saw that it was *me* who Jesus was describing when he said, "It is easy to love those who love you — even hypocrites do that." Then I had to face the truth of his subsequent words: "It is far better to love those who do not love you."

I saw that the path of love I had been treading was a narrow one. I had spent most of my first twenty-one years almost exclusively with people I liked, or who were like me, or who I wanted to like me. If you were into The Doors or day-glow posters or hopping into the car late Saturday night and tripping off to Hong Fat's restaurant for Chinese munchies, you were cool. If not, well, maybe there was hope for you, someday. And if you didn't hang out at the student center snack bar or the girls' dormitory lounge (my two major subjects in college), you had no existential validity. Descartes said, "I think — therefore I am." As I saw the universe from my college view, "I am in a fraternity — therefore I am."

When I entered graduate school, however, the universe was ready to nudge me through the gates of some new mansions. As I took my place in one of my first classes, I found myself sitting next to a woman named Bea, who was conspicuous to me by her age. She must have been at least forty years older than I, at least! Immediately I went into culture shock. Anyone who I hadn't seen at a fraternity party was like an extraterrestrial to me, and my encounter with Bea was like Elliot's blood-curdling discovery of E.T. in the bushes. I just couldn't figure out what someone with horn-rimmed glasses was doing on my side of the teacher's desk. Then, when Bea asked me to call her by her first name, I was tremendously disoriented. Until then, every girl I had met in college was a potential date, but when it came to Bea, I couldn't think of any place I could take her except the reading room of the public library. Not only that, but she was my partner in our work group, and she even spoke to me about her personal life. What to do?

What to do was to discover that Bea was not really different than I. After a few weeks of relating to Bea as my mother, I had the great pleasure of finding her as my friend. This was a marvelous experience for me, as my world became so much richer when I allowed her into it. As I came to know Bea as a delightful person, I realized what a gift it was to be thrown into a situation where I had to face someone who I otherwise would not have been with. I began to understand that the safety of the familiar is not always healthy, and that challenge holds a promise that the comfortable cannot bestow.

As my friendship with Bea unfolded, I realized that the only reason I did not see her as my friend from the start was that I had created a distance between us by my belief in age as a real thing. There is really no difference between any of us — age, skin color, religion, body type, personal history — that is as powerful as our holy sameness. That oneness, called by some people "The *I* that is *We*," is the foundation of all friendship. Friendships are not accidents that happen to us when we are lucky, but gifts of love that we accept by opening our hearts to the love that another person wants to share with us. Hugh Prather, in his *Notes to Myself**, wrote, "*Letting other people in is largely a matter of not spending the energy to keep them out.*" The secret of making friends is the realization that everyone is a potential friend, and then discovering the unique lovable qualities that each person has to offer. We don't need to *make* friends; all we have to do is *accept* them.

---

*Hugh Prather, *Notes to Myself: My Struggle to Become a Person*, Bantam, 1970.

This acceptance is the key to rewarding human relationships, and it can be summed up in one powerful affirmation of six words, like six points of a shining star:

I HAVE FAITH IN YOUR GOODNESS

I have faith in your goodness. This affirmation is a gift to transform those situations in which we are prone to believe another's intentions to be ill. In such a case we must work through that situation until the light is revealed. I am not suggesting that we foolishly allow ourselves to be deceived. (Jesus advised us to be "as gentle as sheep, and as clever as serpents.") I am referring to those daily interactions in which we begin to feel that a friend or business associate is trying to victimize us. Sometimes we read hostility into a peaceable situation, and we are prone to create enmity through simple misunderstanding. These are the moments when we need to affirm God's presence.

Let me give you an example. As a child, I was taught that auto mechanics are dishonest and that they take advantage of needy customers at their mercy. Now, this may be true of some mechanics, but it is certainly not true of all mechanics, and this was a lesson I needed to learn.

It was only fitting, then, that about a year ago my car began to stall at intersections, and I took it into a local service station to be repaired. The owner, Joe, told me that the carburetor needed to be rebuilt, for which I gave him the go-ahead, at a cost of about $120. I chalked up the bill to necessity, and several days later I drove the car out of the station, relieved that the car would once again be working dependably.

You can imagine my chagrin when, a few days later, the car began to conk out exactly as it did before the costly repair. Immediately my old pictures about auto mechanics' shams flashed through my mind. I pictured Joe turning one screw for a moment and then fudging the entire bill. Maybe he just kicked the tire and pronounced the job done. Or maybe he didn't do anything to the car and simply took his girlfriend to the beach for the afternoon. Those were the kinds of thoughts that ran through my head, which led me to the idea of dashing to the bank and stopping payment on the check. Then I imagined being too late and going to the station and finding Joe cackling a sinister laugh, cash in hand. If he did that, I thought, I would call the Better Business Bureau and have him arrested. All of these sweet and delightful thoughts went through my mind in just a few moments, and my immediate impulse was to storm back into Joe's station, call him a few choice names, and threaten him with a lawsuit for malpractice.

Then, as I was about to pull a quick U-turn and make a bee-line for the station, I began to hear a still, small voice within me, calling to me through those churning emotions like the gentle melody of a flute wafting through a tempest of kettle drums. That voice said, *"Wait a bit, Alan . . . Cool off before you go back there."* It was just such a moment that inspired Dale Carnegie, the brilliant mentor and author of one of the most successful books ever written[1], to advise:

> *Whenever you are confronted with some specific problem —*
> *such as handling a child, winning a [spouse] to your way*
> *of thinking, or satisfying an irritated customer, hesitate*
> *about doing the impulsive thing. That is usually wrong.*[2]

The wisdom of this counsel is akin to that of Chief Seneca, who suggested, *"The best cure for anger is delay."*

I decided to wait a day before I went back to Joe.

During that day I had time to think more clearly about the situation. It occurred to me that it was possible that Joe did not intentionally fail on the job, and that he might have just made an error in diagnosing the cause of the problem. In fact, Joe might have even been an O.K. guy, as I like to think of myself, who did the best he could. Then I began to think of the errors that I have made in my work, and I considered the different ways that people have approached me to correct them. I thought of how I felt when someone blasted me for my ineptness, and I remembered that my response was usually to blast them right back. Then I thought of those who corrected me kindly without making me feel like a nincompoop, and I realized I was eager to make these considerate people happy by rectifying my error. As I pondered on how I might deal with Joe, I saw that I had a clear-cut choice before me: either I assume that Joe is a cheat and I go back and threaten him,

---

[1]Dale Carnegie, *How to Win Friends and Influence People*, Pocket Books, 1936, 1964.

[2]Mr. Carnegie also wrote of a European army which required any angry soldier to wait one day before filing a complaint. If a soldier did not wait twenty-four hours (during which he could "sleep on it and cool down") before acting on a grievance, he was punished.

or I could assume that until otherwise proven, his intentions were honorable, and I could go back and speak to him with respect and kindness.

The more I thought about the choice, the better I felt about the way of respect. So I went back to Joe and explained the situation to him in a very easy-going way, leaving out the part about the lawsuit and what my uncle told me about auto mechanics when I was kid. And do you know what was Joe's response to my flexibility? "Gee, I'm really sorry that happened . . . No problem . . . My work is guaranteed. Just bring the car in tomorrow and I'll correct it."

Wow! Was I glad I didn't jump on him without giving him a chance. I shuddered to think of how it might have turned out if I stomped in screaming and yelling. I realized that my willingness to give Joe the benefit of the doubt gave him the opportunity to be kind to me in return. As I left the gas station that day, I felt a joyful peace that no turbulent emotion could offer. I had dumped an old, binding, suffering-causing program and replaced it with a new and far more useful one: *I have faith in your goodness.* It was a turning point in my growth, one which I happily report to you.

There is a delightful P.S. to this story. Because Joe had won my trust, I took him as my regular mechanic. Our mutual understanding developed, and he went on to perform many mechanical favors for me, beyond the call of normal business. As Joe and I became friends, I learned of his life, which was not basically different than my own in terms of the satisfaction and harmony that he wanted for himself. The icing on the cake was that one day, as I was walking into the service station, Joe's assistant, Dom, approached me, eagerly asking, "What do you do for a living, Alan? You've got to tell me . . . I just have to know!" A little taken aback by his zealousness, I answered, "Sure . . . I teach meditation and relaxation."

"I knew it!" Dom exclaimed, "I knew it! . . . I knew there was something peaceful about you . . . I knew it the day you came back when your car wasn't working and you were so patient with Joe. You should see how most people go wild when they feel they've been wronged. They storm in here, shouting and hollering as if they were victims of a scandalous plot . . . But you kept your cool, and that made all the difference."

I chuckled to myself as I decided whether I should tell Dom how close I came to being one of those hooting and hollering people. But that time I wasn't; I was saved by one moment of listening to a still, small voice that said, *"Try to have faith in that man's goodness"* — the voice of a new possibility for loving.

Sometimes these new possibilities come to us in the most amazing ways. Mrs. Jorgensen was an elderly woman I met in a nursing home. She was very old, she had no legs or teeth, her eyes were bloodshot, and she involuntarily stuck her tongue out and in every few seconds. The first time I saw her I was very uneasy about her appearance; I gave her a polite smile and stepped past her as quickly as I could. I just didn't want to face her.

As I would see Mrs. Jorgensen from week to week, I began to be less aware of her physical characteristics, and I noticed that I was spending more and more time chatting with her. Then one day after about six months of seeing Mrs. Jorgensen, as I was walking out of her room I realized I had not been at all conscious of her physical features. I had learned to look past her body and into her soul. And what a beautiful soul it was! She had such a lovely smile, always gave a kind word, and when it came time for exercise class, she tried and worked so hard, bending over in her wheelchair to touch the feet she didn't have. Saints, I discovered, are not confined to cloisters and pilgrimages; they live among us, humbly shining the light of love to ease the burdens of those around them. Mrs. Jorgensen was one of these.

Needless to say, I rose in love with Mrs. Jorgensen, and it was not long before I actually looked forward to seeing her each week. As I walked down the hall toward her, I would light up, and we would hug, and I would kiss her on the cheek, and she would kiss me, and I couldn't care less if she stuck her tongue out of her ear; she was beautiful and I loved her, and that was all that mattered.

One day when I went in to see Mrs. Jorgensen, she was very weak. So I just sat by her bed holding her hand, and there was so much love and light in that room I felt as if my soul was being bathed in peace. It was as if everything that I had ever been taught about who is lovable had been thrown out the window, and I experienced what it meant for two souls to meet in a place more real than the body. It was a very special moment.

The next time I came to the hospital I was told that Mrs. Jorgensen had passed on. I was so happy! Without even thinking about it, the first words out of my mouth were, "Wow! That's great!" When I heard myself say that, I thought, "Now that's not the kind of thing you're supposed to say when somebody dies; you're supposed to be sad and serious and say, 'I'm sorry to hear that,' or some other subdued statement." But the truth was that I was not sad or subdued; I rejoiced in what I felt was a great day for my beloved Mrs. Jorgensen. I was thrilled that she was free of that broken down old body and a lonely life that I know she had grown beyond. I knew that her spirit was alive and smiling, and I knew, too, that the disappearance of her flesh made absolutely no difference in our relationship, for I was as much in love with her after her death as before. It was as if I was given the gift of experiencing her liberation with her, and for that, my cherished friend, I thank you.

This, I believe, is the gift of all the persons we know, and indeed all that we have ever known. We are constantly being given opportunities to look beyond surface appearances until we discover the treasure of the inner person, which shines more beautifully than any physical body. The physical body is the vessel for the expression of the soul, and it can be only as beautiful as the amount of God-Light that radiates through it. I have seen men and women with the most perfect model-like physical features, but because they do not allow their inner beauty to be freely expressed, they are not attractive. On the other hand, I have seen persons who, by the world's standards, are not handsome or pretty, but because the light of their being is shining in full force, they are dynamically attractive and among the most loved of persons.

I was given an exciting insight on this subject by Maurice B. Cooke, the author/channel of the powerful and popular *Hilarion Series*, who explained to me the higher purpose of the popularity of our cuddly alien friend, E.T. Mr. Cooke's guides explained to him that it was no accident that E.T. had such an unusual appearance. "The guides of mankind, who oversee humanity's spiritual evolution," explained Mr. Cooke, "purposely inspired the creators of E.T. to give him such a strange body as a test to see if human beings could learn to love a creature with an appearance so different than our own."

I would say that the experiment was a success, and I am overjoyed about it! Within the first two weeks of the movie's release, *E.T.* attracted more persons and box office receipts than any other movie in history, and it went on to gross $240 million between Memorial Day and Labor Day, 1982. At the Cinerama Dome in Los Angeles, audiences gave standing ovations to the closing credits. The earth fell in love with an alien, and I cannot think of any love affair so healing to our universe.

Perhaps E.T.'s mission can be summed up by the account given to me by a ten-year-old girl: "When he first came on, he looked kind of creepy, and I was scared; but by the end of the movie, I loved him — I mean, he was so cute!"

There is more. When an experiment is a success (especially one of this magnitude), it often bears ramifications beyond those which meet the eye. I would like to share with you a story that reveals an even deeper purpose to E.T.'s huge popularity.

As I was loosening my seat belt on an airplane flying somewhere over Williamsport, Pennsylvania, I found myself seated next to a lovely newlywed couple. Our conversation came around to *E.T.*, and I asked the lady what she thought of the movie.

"There was something special about that picture," she warmly smiled. "It made me feel so happy when I walked out of that theatre . . . I hate to say it, but it was like *a religious experience.*"

Those were her exact words. E.T. was no accident.

Let us consider, too, the recent popularity of the play and movie, *The Elephant Man*, the story of a deformed man who captured the hearts of many persons who at first could not bear to look at him. Could it be that we as a human race are now confronting our age-old bugaboos about physical beauty and the importance of the body? Is it possible that we are finally standing up to the old myths under which we have labored, and having the courage to say, "I love you, no matter what you look like or where you come from or what you have done"? Could it be that we are discovering some new possibilities for loving?

I think so. I think it is happening, and happening fast, now. I think that the horrors of human conflict and the incredible pain of human separation have forced us to reconsider what life is all about, what is really important, and what it is that we truly cherish in one another. I think that together we are taking a new step in human evolution, a momentous growing up as a family of humankind. It is a spiritual event which has been foretold by all the prophets of old, promised by the great ones, and dreamed of by every human being who has ever laid in bed at night and had a fleeting glimpse of a world of love and the possibility that it could someday be real. That someday is *now.* We are actually seeing the fulfillment of millions of years of human awakening, and it is up to all of us to carry it through its flowering.

The power to heal the planet is in our hands, and God will pour as much light through us as we are willing to shine. We now share a common calling to affirm our freedom from the illusion that we were abandoned on a dark planet millions of light years from home. In a way, we are all Mrs. Jorgensens, Elephant Men, and E.T.'s, for we have become weakened and our light has nearly diminished from our spiritual homesickness. But that is all over now, for like our funny-looking friend with a heart that glows at the promise of reunion, it is time for all of us to phone home.

Divine Relations

When the love in you meets the love in me,
Together we step forward in peace and harmony.
— Sue Daniels

I

Acts

There is a scene in *Grease* that I adore. John Travolta, playing Danny, is telling his tough guy friends about this fantastic girl he met at the beach last summer. She was a beautiful blonde visiting from Australia, but as it is with so many summer romances, he will probably never see her again. What Danny does not know, however, is that Sandy has moved to his home town, where she will be attending high school with him. A few days into the school year, in an unsuspecting moment, Sandy taps Danny on the shoulder and says, "Hi!" For a moment — for a fleeting moment — Danny is caught off guard. He softens and we can see the gentleness in his face as he lights up. Danny is genuinely happy to see her, his heart has come alive. But alas, the openness of his affection lasts for just a moment, for he has an image to maintain. Immediately Danny shrugs his shoulders under his motorcycle jacket and mumbles, "Oh, yeah, hi, how ya doin'?" as if she were just an unimportant passing acquaintance. It's his act.

The truth of our relationships is that we want to feel love; the pretense that we don't care is a lie. Danny couldn't express his affection for Sandy because he had an image to protect, a facade that was unreal and completely flimsy, yet powerful enough — through his fear of losing it — to stand between him and all the love he really wanted to feel and express. Like Sandy, the people in our lives are literally aching — even dying — to feel love from us, and yet, like Danny, we hold it back for reasons we can't really explain. This is the human masquerade, the charade of life that makes apathy seem real and love an

123

impossible dream, while love is the only life great enough to bear the beams of Truth, and separateness a dark dream that has never been substantiated. Though we may be quick to declare, "I don't care what she thinks of me," our hearts are yearning for a communion that we once knew, but learned to deny. As Dr. Leo Buscaglia so genuinely affirms, "We are *all* lovers!"

I had my own experience of a "Greasey" kind of act when I went to visit my cousin's wife, Ilona, in the hospital. Ilona is a woman who has gone through a rather tough life, and in response she has built a rigid shell around herself, allowing expressions of love in and out at only certain personal times. I confess that I have sometimes felt put off by her hardened exterior and allowed myself to believe that she was not reachable. When I went to see her in the hospital, however, the person I found in that bed was nothing like the one I knew outside. She had just come back from surgery, and while still under the euphoric influence of the anaesthesia she allowed herself to be soft and gentle. She took my hand, lovingly stroked my arm, and told me how much she appreciated our friendship. She was as warm and cuddly and giving as the most huggable person I know, and I deeply enjoyed a very rich and real contact with her.

In those few moments, Ilona gave up her act. She gave herself permission to let the caring, affectionate little girl in her come out, for *that*, you see, was the real Ilona. The tough, ornery one was just a cover-up. I have not forgotten those open moments with Ilona, and now if I start to feel distant from her I recall those precious minutes and I remember the beauty of who she really is — whether she is showing it or not.

In the movie *Resurrection* there is a scene that draws this lesson into broader blossom. Ellen Burstyn plays a simple woman named Anna Mae whose father is an extremely cold, hardened man. His pain in life has been so great that he has walled himself away from everyone, unwilling to forgive anyone, including — and especially — himself.

In the movie we find him on his deathbed, with Anna Mae at his side. Anna Mae, who once died on the operating table and returned to life with a memory of the heaven world, is very open to the spiritual life. She tells her dad that there is a glorious world beyond this one and he has nothing to worry about; he will be guided and cared for. She assures him, too, that she loves him no matter what their estranged lives have been, and she appreciates him very much. Meanwhile the old man just lies there, stern and callous as ever.

A few days later, however, his time is come. As he is about to pass on he begins to see the next world opening before him. Suddenly the harsh lines disappear from his face, his lips open into a boyish smile, he lifts his head and softly exclaims, "The light! . . . The light!"* Anna Mae, at his side, begins to weep tears of joy, affirming, "Yes, Daddy! The light! Isn't it beautiful!" Moments later the old man dies peacefully.

This moving scene caused me to think, "That man went through almost an entire life of misery and hiding, and he experienced but one moment of peace at its very end." How sad, I thought, that he held back the expression of his real, sensitive self for so long. It was a lesson to me that I must not wait until I am on my deathbed to enjoy the experience of love. I want to live every moment of life to its fullest. I don't want to wait until my last few moments to be who I am. I think that we can all be who we are — indeed we must — now, if we are willing to open our hearts to the kind of relationships we really want.

All the love that is waiting for us at the end of our life is available to us in full measure now. Jesus told of the king who invited many of his friends to a great feast (symbolizing the Kingdom of Heaven). Everyone had an excuse, something they just had to do before they could come. ("One to his farm, one to his business.") So he went into town and invited the simple and the poor and the hungry, who accepted because they had nothing they had to do first. They had no acts to uphold before they could enter the Golden Kingdom.

Some of the most dramatic experiences of acts falling away are those that I have had in human relations workshops. In these retreats persons from all walks of life gather together with the commitment to trust and be open and be who we really are. On Friday evening, most of us usually sit around trying to project an image, like "I'm cool," or "Don't touch me — I'm fragile," or "I'm a nice guy," or "I'm invulnerable." Then, as the group members begin to feel safe and let go, the acts fall away and the persons behind the acts allow their real selves — their genuinely beautiful selves — to emerge. As facades are cast by the wayside, honest feelings are shared and there grows a sense of

---

*When the great visionary William Blake left his world he was singing songs of praises of the angels he saw coming to meet him.

of communication and oneness that is a thousand times more fulfilling than the games and roles that most of us play in the outer world. It gradually becomes obvious that who we really are is far more thrilling and satisfying than any facade we could fabricate. By Sunday afternoon something happens, something which I cannot really explain, a rare, even miraculous event that reminds me that life is indeed precious, worth living. It is the merging of twelve half-empty human beings into one whole, living, loving, spiritually-endowed Force. It is the birth of the soul into joyous expression, the transformation of Children of God from slumber to aliveness, and the fulfillment of the prayer, "on earth as it is in heaven."

I remember one such group of us sitting in our circle on Sunday afternoon, and I tell you it felt as if there was just one big bathtub of love in that room, a universal womb that we all shared. There was nothing to be ashamed of, nothing hidden, nothing to fear. We had removed our masks, spoken the truth, and out of our willingness to grow, blossomed mutual appreciation and the deepest, most genuine caring. In that moment what had begun as an experiment in human relations had been transfigured into a sacrament of Divine Relations.

II

Transformation

We can use this awakening as a starting point to see how we can transform all of our human relationships into divine ones. Relationships have played an emotionally significant role in my life, and it seems that they are an important issue for many of us. I feel that this is because we want so badly for our relationships to work, and too often they haven't. As spiritual beings, we hunger for the life of the spirit, and when we aren't feeling fulfilled, we have to do something about it. So we go through all kinds of books, classes, therapies, workshops, affirmations, and gurus to make those relationships work. And rightfully they should work! God gave our lives to us in perfect working order. If any aspect of our livelihood is not reflecting Divinity, we must look into it until we see where more light needs to be shined on it. Like Jacob in the dark forest, we must wrestle with the angel until we win a blessing. We must courageously face the truth of our relationships as they are now, so we may know how we need to change the way we are approaching them. Such honesty is a requirement for lifting our relationships into the rewarding love for which they were given to us.

Let's begin with the issue of *commitment*. "Commitment" is one of the most often spoken words these days, and it is also almost always misused and probably the least understood. I have grappled with the issue of commitment for a long time, and I would like to share with you what I have experienced and what I now feel that commitment is about.

I can remember relationships in which I spent hours — I mean *hours* and *hours* — of long telephone conversations with women on the subject, "Should we be committed to one another?" I ran up enormous telephone bills, imbibed fantastic quantities of herb tea in Greenwich Village cafes, and wrote and rewrote long, heartful letters on new age stationary over the question, "What does it mean to be committed to one another?" The issue usually includes, "Am I willing to be committed to you?" "Do I really want you to be committed to me?" "What will happen to my life if I commit myself to you; what will I have to give up, and what will I gain?" "Will one or both of us get hurt?" "Am I really capable of committing myself to anyone?" And so on. One summer I went cross-country with a girlfriend, and we spent five out of the six weeks discussing whether or not we wanted to be committed to one another. I missed the Rockies, the Grand Canyon, and Big Sur because I was so busy discussing our relationship that I forgot to look out the window. As you may know, this business of discussing commitment can sometimes lead to commitment — not to a person, but to a mental institution!

There *must* be some way to see the light through this issue of commitment, and here is what I have found it to be: *There is only one real possible commitment that any human being can make — the commitment to God*, or spiritual growth or awakening. To attempt to commit ourselves to anyone or anything other than God would not only be foolish, but impossible. Of course we have hesitation about vowing our allegiance to a spouse or lover above all else; that is offering all of our self to a very limited piece of the universe, and no one wants to restrict themselves in such a narrow way. No relationship can work if the other partner is the be-all and end-all of our commitment.

Ah, but here is the great promise that lifts all relationships into a higher purpose and not only makes commitment to a human being possible, but elevates it to its loftiest potential. If I have committed myself to God, I am free to commit myself to another person in a way that creates the deepest kind of love between two human beings. Because my happiness is not dependent on you, I am free to love and serve you in the most joyous, exciting, and most rewarding way; I am free to give you *all* my love because, through my foundation in God, I know that *the more love I give, the more I have to give.*

God does not ask us to give up anything; He merely asks that we keep Him first in our heart. Yes, at first we must surrender our *attachment*, which sometimes requires that we physically or emotionally let go of a person or thing, and always requires that we be *willing* to let go if that is what God asks of us. But once we have decided that it is really God that we want, God will return the person (or another in her/his place, if that is for our highest good) to us, this time with His blessings. In such a case it is not an "either God or something"; after we have chosen God first, it is God *and* something, or more exactly, God *in* or *through* something. Then we are free to enjoy it, for only then can we live without fear of losing it. Once we know that we have God whether or not we have this person, we live in a state of peace. And that is the only possible foundation for a healthy and rewarding relationship.

I have found that the highest ideals that I would want to commit myself to in a relationship with one person, I can enjoy with many persons. I was in a relationship in which we got to the point where I was deciding whether or not I wanted to be committed to her. As I was trying to figure out what commitment meant, it occurred to me that most of the rewards to be gained from being committed to one person could be gained many times over by applying those same values to *all* of my relationships. This may at first seem as if I am advocating "free love" — and indeed I am, for the nature of love is that it must always be free. The free love that I honor, however, is not a life of physical or emotional promiscuity, for such a form of love seeks mainly to take, and so cannot bring the peace that we yearn to know. The love that I stand for is the Divinely free love that seeks to give and share and finds delight in the happiness of the beloved. This kind of loving enjoys a commitment to the well-being of others before one's self, and expands to bless the whole family of humanity at no cost to any particular relationship. It is the kind of love that shines like the sun, equally, fully, blessedly, on all.

As I held my relationship with this woman up to my highest ideals for loving, I began to feel that the kind of spiritual fulfillment I was seeking in being committed to her was really a taste of the kind of life I want to live all the time with all persons. Aside from the agreement not to become sexually involved with other women, I could not think of anything I could commit to her that I didn't want to commit to everyone. To me, commitment meant giving her emotional and spiritual support when she needed it, being honest with her, encouraging her to succeed in her aspirations, accepting her love in the way she uniquely expressed it, forgiving her, hanging in there when the going got tough, and loving her unconditionally. The more I thought about it, it just seemed odd to say, "Because I am committed to you I will forgive you or love you more unconditionally than everyone else." That kind of commitment seemed to me to manufacture a kind of separation that somehow demeaned all of my other human interactions by placing them in a category that made it okay for me not to give one hundred percent to them because I was not committed to them as I was committed to someone else. Somehow that notion of moral division did not feel totally right to me. What did feel right was to strive to commit myself to see-ing God equally in all persons and giving everyone the fullest love that I know how to give. I knew that I could do it because pure love is in-finite and it is not diminished — in fact, it is increased — by its giving. It became clear to me that what I wanted to commit myself to was a life founded on the celebration of God, and I could do that with or without a special partner.

There is, of course, great value to be gained through a deep and committed relationship with another person. In such a relationship the agreement to support one another encourages a loving trust that opens the door to rich personal growth, as both partners can feel free to share their intimate selves with one another. At the same time, because both persons share the same physical, emotional, and mental space, the fire of interpersonal friction is hotter, and there are many valuable oppor-tunities to learn to let go of self-centeredness for the sake of harmoniz-ing with the mate. This combination of trust and working through dif-ficulties creates a womb for nurturing a love that deepens and mellows over time in a powerful way that lighter relationships do not.

Someone who does not commit him- or herself to an exclusive rela-tionship grows just as meaningfully through different kinds of ex-periences. While the married couple experiences the joys and struggles of having their lives so intimately interwoven, the person who chooses to go it alone goes through the challenges and freedoms of not having someone with him or her most of the time. He or she must deal with feelings of aloneness, sexual desires, family expectations, and more subtly — and even more critically — the tendency to escape into a seemingly safe (but dangerously sterile) world of unchallenged self. Such a retreat may be useful for a short period of time, but in the long run escape is not healthy, and the rivers of destiny will always push such a person back into the thick of human interaction, for the purpose of living is not to rest on one's complacency, but to grow into unity with all of the human family. Yet, as the unmarried person learns to deal with and conquer these challenges, she or he will eventually emerge triumphant, worthy of enjoying the strength of self-mastery.

Both paths of life, marriage and singlehood, bear their own advantages and detractions. If we look at them closely, however, we see that they are more alike than they are different, for they are united by one common purpose: *Self-discovery*. Wherever we go, we find only ourself, and the joyous lessons of Self-discovery are equally available in marriage and singlehood. On the New Jersey Turnpike there is a point at which the highway divides into two roads: buses go to one side, and cars to the other. Then the roads run parallel for a number of miles, and both lanes have the same entrances, exits, and rest stops. Later on down the Turnpike both sides of the highway merge again into one great thoroughfare. So it is with the paths of marriage and singlehood; they are not separate, but simply different lanes of the same highway of personal growth. No matter which road we take, we have to pay the same tolls and we end up at the same destination.

The two ways of living are actually different aspects of the same diamond truth of life: *We are all married to everyone, and we are all ultimately alone.* Walt Whitman hiked out into the country, took a deep breath of life, and wrote, *"I celebrate myself!"* When I read these words a hundred years later, his poem was a gift to me like a newly-wed spouse leaving me a love note when she left for work in the morning before I got up. And when one of my brothers a hundred miles up the coast spills a barrage of oil that pollutes a sparkling beach and renders it lifeless, it is like a thoughtless husband who leaves his greasy tools in the kitchen sink. We are all united in a great marriage of humankind that makes the Brady Bunch household seem as mellow as a yogi's Himalayan cave by comparison.

At the same time we are all very much alone. Each of us must make our own decisions and no one else can live our life for us. We can abnegate our self-responsibility and let other people decide our lives for us, but we are responsible for giving them the power to do so, and for following their suggestions. Spiritual teachers, masters, and guides can show us the correct road, but we must walk it ourselves. We are accountable for every experience we undergo. I once insulted an employer by making a poor joke about him to his face. Later that day I realized I had to apologize to him, and I had to do it myself. Yes, I could have asked someone else to do it for me, but eventually I would have had to look my boss in the eye myself. So it is with all our acts and relationships: no matter how much or how long we have avoided owning our lives, we must sooner or later look life squarely in the eye, and we might as well do it now. This is the aloneness that we must accept. Assuming such right responsibility brings great triumph, for on the other side of the fear of aloneness is the incomparable joy of self-completeness. When we add one "L" (which stands for "Love") to "alone," we get *all one* — the real idea behind "alone" and the crowning freedom to which aloneness ultimately leads. When we realize that we must go it alone, we automatically know that we *can* go it alone, and there is no greater sense of fulfillment than this one.

The point of life is not to be married or single — it is to *be*. We are human *beings*, or humans being. It does not matter so much what lifestyle we choose — it's *what we make of the opportunities to grow*, that counts. All single and married people have an abundant wealth of opportunities to transform separateness into sharing, to discover One where there seemed to be two. I don't believe that when we get to Heaven God will ask us, "Were you in a relationship or did you go it alone?" He will ask, *"Were you true to yourself and were you a light to the world in treading the path of your heart's bidding?"*

No matter what style of life in which we find ourselves, we must know that we are in exactly the right place for our ideal evolution. When doubts about our place in life begin to assail us, we need to remember that we have created our circumstances to awaken us for our highest good. That is the awareness that makes all relationships — or lack of them — Divine, for it is the grandest way of looking at life, the way that keeps God first in our hearts.

Keeping all this in mind, I would like to share with you what I feel are the three basic ingredients for making our human relations Divine. These are the principles that have helped me the most, and I offer them to you with my confidence in their power to transform *all* lives by virtue of the truth contained within them.

1. KEEP ON LOVING, NO MATTER WHAT.

When the disciples asked Jesus, "How many times shall we forgive? . . . Seven?" the master answered, "Nay, *seventy times seven.*" The most effective way to create and keep a precious relationship is to *appreciate the basic goodness of the other person, no matter what mistakes they make.* I believe that it is so important to keep on letting go, forgiving, giving support, overlooking errors, and continuously recognizing the unique beauty that only she or he brings into the world as a gift for all. As I reflect on the persons who have loved me even when I acted selfishly or foolishly, I realize that holding to the vision of every soul's sparkling perfection is the highest gift I could, in turn, offer to others. Blessing and appreciation are the same. *Appreciation is not something that happens to us; it is an act that we do, a way of living that we choose.* When I am tempted to feel hurt, slighted, or vengeful, I ask myself, *"Would I rather have this feeling, or love?"* The answer is always obvious. Hugh Prather captures the essence of personal growth in one choice: *"Right or Happy?"* That question condenses all human experience into a clear decision: Is it more important for me to feel holier or more righteous than another person, or would I rather enjoy the warmth of a loving relationship? I am seeing that my sense of joy and satisfaction in life greatly depends on how much I put forgiveness into action.

2. SEE THE WORLD FROM THE OTHER PERSON'S POINT OF VIEW.

This lesson was taught to me in a dramatic way at a workshop on relationships. The leader asked us to think of someone close to us with whom we were not getting along, and then to jot down an outline of the key turning points of that person's life. Wow! . . . What an eye-opener! I was feeling irked about a woman who I felt was overly preoccupied with money. As I wrote down what I knew about her life, I began to realize why she is that way. She spent her early years in a poor foreign country, in a family of ten children in which everyone got just a little bit of the little the family had. Her early life was a continuous struggle for what you and I take for granted as the simple necessities of life. Then I imagined what it must have been like to come to this country after experiencing such a barren childhood, and here find some money to buy the things she needed. It all became very clear to me. I realized that *if I had gone through the same experience, I would have acted exactly as she did.* There is a Native American proverb, *"Never judge a man until you've walked a mile in his moccasins."* After having walked for just ten minutes in this woman's moccasins, I experienced a deeply compassionate understanding for her life, and I realized how shallow it was of me to judge her.

3. WANT FOR THE OTHER PERSON WHAT THEY WANT FOR THEMSELVES.

When I was just starting out as an assistant human relations trainer, my supervisor and friend Arlene King gave me a gift I will never forget: *"Alan, I would be very happy to be associated with you professionally someday."* She knew my dream and she built a bridge of love by sharing it with me. When we pray for others to get what they want, we participate in Grace. One night I made a prayer list entitled, *"If I had the power to give anyone anything."* Then I recorded the names of whoever came to my mind, and next to each one I wrote a one or two word description of what I would give them if I could. I did not write what *I* thought they should have, but what *they* wanted for themselves. The list included good health, a vacation in the Bahamas, a toy truck, midwife's equipment, and complete God-realization. As I came to see life through each of these persons' eyes, I felt warmly close, even akin to every one of them, and I was lifted into a oneness that brought a flow of love that I usually do not feel when I pray for myself.

Dr. Jerry Jampolsky, author of the very popular *Love is Letting Go of Fear**, gave a dramatic demonstration of the

---

*Jerry Jampolsky, *Love is Letting Go of Fear*, Bantam, 1981.

power of "outward thinking." He asked a large audience, "Would you like to be free of your troubles?" When the group responded with a bright "Yes!" he invited everyone in the meeting hall to send love to Joey, a little boy with cancer on stage with him. Within moments the atmosphere of that room became light and clear, and a great healing energy filled the auditorium. Everyone's troubles had disappeared, for the law of consciousness is such that our minds can hold only one thought at a time, and when we pray for someone else, our own little troubled self has no reality, and we are free.

All of the principles of healing relationships boil down to three holy ideas: *oneness, consideration,* and *love.* When we realize that other people have the same feelings we do, it becomes easy to know how to treat them. This is the secret of unraveling even the most complex jangle of human relations. Many years ago Jesus taught the same principle, and we call it *"The Golden Rule."* And rightfully so, for that is what it is: a holy prescription for healing broken hearts. *Every hard relationship is healable*; we just have to know how to apply the cure. Remembering that the other person is the same as us is the truth that restores peace to our lives.

The way to wholeness is surprisingly simple. Perhaps our many ideas, concepts and analyses have served only to complicate our journey through human relationships and obscure our vision of a simple, clear-cut path. All we need to remember is that we can make ourselves and each other happy by thinking of what we would like from others, and then give exactly that to them. Herein lies the simple answer to many complicated questions.

III
Deciding to Love

I would like to — I must — conclude this very important chapter by sharing with you a marvelous miracle which I have been blessed to experience. It is an awakening that has completely changed my life, an insight with a potential so great that I would like every person to know about it, for I believe that every life can be transformed by putting this principle into action. What I am about to describe is a healing vision that releases emotional wounds and makes them disappear as if they never existed, replacing them with a deep confidence in our ability to love and be loved. I would like to share with you a formula for healing relationships and transforming them into a living love so bright that we see all of our relationships in the holy light in which they were created.

For many years I have heard Hilda counsel men and women going through a troubled time in a marriage or relationship. Her advice to them is usually the same: she asks them, "Can you remember when you first fell in love with him or her? Can you think of some special moments when you felt so delighted and united with your partner that you were filled with gratitude that they were a part of your life? Can you remember the first time you said, 'I love you?' "

Just about everyone can remember such a moment, and I would see their faces light up as they thought of it. Then Hilda would say, "Go home and keep thinking and feeling about your partner in this way. Tune into those wonderful feelings you enjoyed when you looked into his or her eyes and really adored one another. Then act toward them as you did then: call them 'Honey'; give them a big hug when they come home; do something special for them that lets them know how much you care. Then, as you nourish the feelings that make those memories so precious, your love will be renewed and it will flower into a new relationship even more fulfilling than before."

Again and again I heard Hilda give this advice, and again and again I heard people come back weeks or months later and say, "I just want to thank you for your idea ... I tried what you suggested and it worked! . . . Things are so much better between us now, and I am so grateful!"

I was thrilled to see these healings of the spirit taking place around me; the freedom and new enthusiasm in these people's eyes were a gift to behold. Somehow, though, Truth becomes real only when we experience it first-hand, and I did not realize the power of this method until I tried it for myself.

There was a woman who I fell — and rose — in love with, years ago. For a while we were a couple, and then we parted with some bitterness. The relationship was not resolved, and to me it remained a dark spot in my consciousness, a kind of eclipse of the light of my soul. When I thought about Laura, all I remembered was the hurt I had felt, and my mind dwelt on thoughts of what I felt was her unkindness to me. When I would occasionally see her after we had separated, all I could think of were the struggles I went through in trying to find peace with her, and these meetings were awkward and uncomfortable. Though we had physically parted, I was still tied to her by my memories and the emotional fuel I was giving them.

The relationship was begging for healing, and I did not know how to accomplish it. When I saw Laura I tried to be extra kind and loving, but somehow when there is subconscious unrest, outer facades to the contrary seem only to magnify the inner turmoil. I would smile and be polite and say nice things to her, but inwardly I was just waiting for the moment when I could find an excuse to leave the room. I read articles on relationships, tried to send her love through the ethers, meditated, contemplated, and prayed to God for assistance to get me out of this ordeal, but it seemed as if I wasn't getting anywhere. As time went on, all I wanted was for this relationship to be healed.

Then I decided to try what I had heard Hilda tell so many other people to do. I *decided to love* Laura. One morning it became so clear to me that the only way out of this mess was to just start loving Laura fully and completely, and not to allow any thoughts of resentment or emptiness to creep into even one moment of my consciousness. I decided to commit myself to loving her. It wasn't a commitment to her as if to be married or together as man and woman; it was a commitment to appreciating the perfect beauty in Laura, the Light that I loved and honored as a special ray of goodness in a dark world. The commitment took the form of a silent vow that whenever Laura's name or face came into my mind, I would immediately and purposefully surround it with all the loving thoughts I could think about her, showering her image in my heart with thankfulness for the gift of her friendship.

As the strength of this decision rippled through me, my soul was bolstered in a way that can only be described as the union of man's effort and God's Grace. I remembered how my friend T.D. described his winning freedom from alcoholism: "One day it just clicked within me that there was *absolutely no question* about whether or not I could take another drink. Before that I had thought, 'maybe I won't,' or 'well, one drink wouldn't hurt,' or 'just socially, maybe,' but this time I knew — I just *knew* — that whether or not I could take a drink was not even an issue; there was no discussion about it, no debating, no considering, no weighing. It was a one thousand percent absolute necessity with no alternative. That moment I knew I was finished with alcoholism. My decision was made, and there was no veering from it. In fact, it was not even a decision — it was a fact of life."

That was how I felt about healing my relationship with Laura — there was no doubt in my mind that I could do anything other than love her completely, wholly, and unconditionally. That was the fact of life, the way it had to be. I knew this was the only answer to my prayers; I could no longer afford to sit around and wait for God to do it for me. I knew that God would help me, and I saw what I would have to do to win God's Grace: I would have to commit myself to loving Laura — one thousand percent.

I sat down, closed my eyes, and began to think of the *positive* memories I had about Laura. I remembered how much I enjoyed her kooky sense of humor; I thought about the first time we took a walk in the park together; I remembered how nice it was to share so many interests and aspirations; and I laughed to picture those imaginative little notes she wrote me, the ones with little hand-drawn cartoons which she would leave for me to find on my refrigerator door. As I remembered these thoughtful acts, I began to recall many other kindnesses that she had shown me, ones that I had forgotten because my consciousness was so preoccupied with memories of pain. I was amazed to remember all of these *good* things about her, and I even felt a little foolish for having allowed myself to forget them.

Then the healing came. As I focused on these pleasant memories, a great wave of appreciation — genuine thankfulness — for Laura welled up in my heart, and *I began to feel just like I did when we first met.* I began to think of her as my good friend, and I started to feel all the trust and support and excitement that we had enjoyed years ago. It was as if I was transported back into a garden of delight of being with her, one that I had somehow strayed from. And did it feel good! God, it felt so much better and freer and righter than those dark thoughts of bitterness that I had allowed to color my consciousness. I had found my way home.

I was in love with Laura again. Actually, it was not "again," for with this love came the awareness that *I had never been out of love with her.* The love I felt when we first met and the love I felt now were the same love; the love never stopped during those years of turbulent emotions. The love was constant and the distance was a big mistake, a bad dream. The negative feelings were just a smoke screen that temporarily obscured the love but could never replace it. I understood that my love for Laura was real — in fact, *love was the only truth of our relationship* — and the hurt, a lie.

What I saw, too, was that all of the hurtful experience was also a part of love — God's love to get me free. As I rose in love with Laura again, you see, I no longer had the infatuated illusions that I had the first time, like wanting to possess her and have her be totally committed to me, and having a lifetime of non-stop hugging. Miraculously (and quite cleverly on the part of God), my hard times with Laura had burned those notions out of my consciousness and left me with a much purified love for my friend, my sister in God, Laura. All I wanted to do now was love her, and what she did in return did not really matter. Loving her, appreciating her, and being thankful for her were quite enough.

This reawakening of my love for Laura was so powerful that I knew I had to tell her of it. Immediately I got up and sprinted to the telephone. As I picked up the receiver, however, the mind — that divinely pesky and mischievous critter, playing the game of the slayer of the real — clicked into action. I began to have thoughts like, "Will she really believe me?" and "What if I make a fool of myself?" and "I sure hope this doesn't get me involved with her again!" and a barrage of similar thoughts. But because I knew that my love was real and the doubts imposters, I refused to allow them to stop me. When love begins to move, there is no stopping it. When the power of God says, "Go!" there is no force in the universe that can resist.* I dialed her number and told her, without any perfunctory small talk, "Hi Laura, this is Alan. I love you very much and I appreciate you more than I can say, and I am very glad that you are a part of my life." Period.

There is a verse from the psalms that says, "Take refuge in the Truth, for the Truth never fails." Actually, I don't really know if there is exactly such a verse, or if there is, where it is, but I do know that there must be something like it, because when I said that to her, something very holy happened, something very mighty and more wonderful than a human mind can understand. When I spoke those words to Laura, because they were true, love was awakened in her heart, and we had the clearest, most meaningful conversation we have ever had . . . one that lifted our entire relationship into the Light. Everything I had been wanting and trying to say to her through years

---

*Meher Baba said, "True love is unconquerable and irresistable. It goes on gathering force until it transforms everyone it touches."

of questioning, testing, demanding, tears, rippled emotions, and seeking love, was completely communicated and resolved in just a few minutes. Sri Ramakrishna said that "even if a room has been dark for many years, it takes just one flick of the right switch to replace all the darkness with light." Jesus said, "Know the Truth and the Truth shall set you free." Because true love had become the foundation of our relationship, we were able to speak clearly with one another, and the truth of what happened between us became perfectly clear. And because Truth is the greatest healer, as we spoke it, both of us and our relationship were instantly healed.

As a fitting postscript to this story, I must tell you that the next time I saw Laura, she came up to me and gave me a great big hug, an affectionate gift that I used to fault her for not doing when we were together. It is said that "You can only enjoy what you let go of," and the healing of my relationship with Laura is a powerful testimony to this wonderful truth.

There is one more miracle I want to share with you, a message of tremendous importance and encouragement for me and, I believe, for you, as well. As I leaf back through the pages of this book, I see that I have described quite a number of difficult and sometimes painful relationships with which I have struggled. As I read over these confessions, my first reaction was, "Maybe I shouldn't include all of these stories; people may think I'm weak or unenlightened or a crummy person to have been involved in so many unkempt human interactions."

But then, as I was deciding whether or not to censor some of them, another voice spoke within me, the voice of the gentle guidance of my higher self. That guiding light said: "*Consider the state of these relationships now.*" So I reflected further, and as I began to focus on what has become of these difficult relationships, I realized that *every single one of them has been healed.* No matter what hurt, separation, or emptiness there was, *every one of these people is now my friend*, and all of these friendships are now living — have grown into — the Light of Love. The essence of this magnificent teaching is, as that inner sage explained, "*It does not matter what these relationships were; it is what they have become that is important.*" As I reflected on these words, I realized that the transformation of these relationships has been the great healing of my life.

Then that voice spoke again:

"This is why you must include all of these stories: precisely because they have been transformed from pain to freedom, from barrenness to love — because they have been healed.

These relationships were given to you for your growth, and as you have prospered from the lessons you have learned from them, it is your responsibility to bear witness to the truth of transformation so that others may see, as you have, that what once seemed to be the reality of pain has been completely replaced by the Truth of Love. The fact that all of these relationships have grown into love is the beacon of hope that will give you and many others the strength and confidence to call upon the invincible power of love — God's love — to heal all of your relationships.

The ability to be healed is God's gift to you, and your work to heal your relationships is your offering to God. Your Heavenly Source needs you to accomplish the transformation you seek for yourself. Now you must realize that God's heart is your heart. All the love you seek to feel and give is available with your willingness to be a channel for it.

The principles of healing relationships are not different than those of healing the body, the mind, or any challenge which presents itself to you. All obstacles can be overcome by lifting them into a new perspective, by recognizing the goodness, the love, the beauty contained within them. Your relationships are excellent teachings for your growth because through resolving them you gain the strength and learn the lessons of a lifetime. It is precisely through the medium of relationships that God teaches you how to heal your entire life and that of your precious planet.

This is the truth that has been begging for your awareness and the golden rule which embraces you and all of your brothers and sisters in the loving arms of Divinity."

Only Love

The truth is that everyone loves everyone.
— Patricia Sun

When I heard Patricia Sun speak these words, I couldn't understand how she could make such a statement. "What about wars and violent crimes and divorces?" I thought to myself. "Surely there is no love in these kinds of acts." Apparently there were other people in the audience who shared my questioning, for as I was pondering on the idea, a man a few rows in front of me raised his hand.

"What you just said reminds me of a friend of mine who I believe is rather egotistical," the fellow stood up and reported. "The other day he told me that he knows that everyone loves him. Don't you think that's a little presumptuous?"

"Not at all!" Patricia answered brightly. "I certainly love him!" she smiled, ". . . and I know he loves me, as well!" Well, that really stepped on the toes of my belief system. How could she say that she and this guy loved each other when they didn't even know one another? My mind went on and on trying to figure out what she meant, and I concluded that she was just trying to be positive or attempting to create love by making believe it was already someplace it was not.

Since that day four years ago, I have thought again and again and again on this idea, and I am beginning to see that there is a lot more to what Patricia Sun said than I originally understood. It may indeed be true that everyone *does* love everyone. It may really be possible that behind all seemingly hurtful, hateful, and negative acts, there lives a Love that is very real — perhaps even more real than the negative emotions we accepted as true. The fact that we don't always see love does not mean it is not there; it just means that we are not looking at life from the highest perspective. When recognized through divine eyes, Love is the guiding force — indeed the *only* Force — in the entire universe. How can this be?

RISING IN LOVE

Several years ago I was seeing a woman named Denise, whom I wanted very much to love me. One winter's afternoon she telephoned me and said, "I just wanted to say 'good-bye' before I leave for California this evening. I woke up this morning with this urge to go see my family, so that's what I'm doing. I should be back in a week or two, I guess."

Upon hearing this I began to get an empty feeling in the pit of my stomach, the kind I used to get in elementary school when they were choosing basketball teams and I was one of the last to be picked. I felt let down and hurt that she didn't ask me to go with her. A bunch of insecurity feelings were stirred up within me, and I felt deserted. I told Denise to have a good time, but my heart was absent from my words.

A couple of days later, I was discussing my experience with another friend. After hearing me describe my feelings of being left out, she asked me, "Do you realize that Denise loves you very much?"

"I don't really think so," I answered. "I don't think she would have gone to California like that if she did."

"But don't you see, silly, that Denise's going to California doesn't mean that she doesn't love you — all it means is that she went to California!"

Well, that was one of the "Aha!" moments of my life. It was one of those realizations that I could not have gotten from reading a thousand books or doing a shoulderstand for twelve hours. It was one of those moments when the pivotal piece of the puzzle fit into place and I saw the truth of the whole matter. The truth was that it was entirely possible that Denise loved me, even if she did go to California. It was only my thoughts, my belief system, my emotional programming that led me to think that her going was not an act of complete love. The moment I realized that, I tell you in one single moment, *the entire scene completely shifted in my mind,* and I felt really fine about Denise going. In fact I was glad that she did, for I knew that it was important to her. I knew that she loved me, so I could enjoy her happiness. Her unlovingness, I discovered, existed only in *my perception,* and as soon as I saw the situation in the right light, it was clear that all there ever was in that whole act was love, only love.

Let's take a few moments now to look our difficult relationships squarely in the eye, that we may see how love can be where it seemed to have been missing.

This is the key principle of healing relationships:

**All human interactions are expressions of the statement
"I want to feel love."**

Some acts are pure expressions of love, such as a Mother Theresa devoting her life to serving the poor and the dying, and some acts are distorted expressions, such as the criminal seeking to gain notoriety as a tough fighter, but all of these actions share the common characteristic of a human being striving to feel a sense of self-worth and importance about his or her life. Everyone wants to feel love; the only difference is in the way we go about finding it.

At the opening session of my first human relations workshop all of the participants were given a white gummed label upon which we were asked to write a short statement about ourselves. Then we were instructed to fix the labels on our foreheads and mill around the room, silently showing and reading one another's statements. There was quite an array of interesting and imaginative notes like, "I'm shy," "I love racquetball," and "I just left a relationship." But the one that said it all, the one that wakes me up like a church bell every time I reflect on it, was the message written by my later-to-be dear friend, Arlene King, who had the courage to write, "*I want you to like me.*" In these six simple but awesomely powerful words, she captured what everyone in the room was trying to express, and boiled all of the camouflaged statements into one honest communication.

If, as Arlene so humbly declared, love is our deepest and most important need, why then do we have such difficulty in asking for it or expressing it? Why did so many of those messages on our foreheads take so many words in so many disguised forms to say something so simple and honest? What is it that causes us to seek love in a thousand different experiences that mirror love, but do not really equal it? How have we become so separated from each other that the most meaningful words of our life, "*I love you,*" are often the most cumbersome to utter? The answer, which belongs to all of us, is one that invites us to take a journey together back into our common origin.

As children we knew how to be in love. We knew no restrictions on whom we could love. Human characteristics like color and age made about as little difference to us as the color or age of our teddy bear. Love is not blind; it is just not petty. Once I, a friend, and a little boy were having lunch in a park in Davenport, Iowa, when the boy disappeared. After searching for him for a while, we found him sitting on a park bench with a group of old men, engaging in deep conversation and intermittently playing his harmonica. He had no concept that old men are different than him. His love knew no bounds.

Then, somewhere along the yellow-brick road of our evolution, we learned an idea called "rejection." Someone told us, "You're a good girl if you color the nose on the clown red, but if you color it green, you're wrong. Or you're stupid. Or you fail. Or if you make a joke while teacher is talking, you have to go stand out in the hall by yourself. Or if you don't go to church, you're going to go to hell. All human definitions of love.

The learned fear of abandonment, the hellish striving to conform to human definitions of love, is exactly the source of our being afraid to ask for love, for if we ask for it and it does not come, we face the sinister illusion of not receiving it. Because we forgot that love is a living Spirit that expands with its expression, we began to treat love as a vulnerable commodity, and we became slaves to the popularly acknowledged but never substantiated myth that "You've got to hide your love away."

We don't have to hide our love away; love was given to us to let it shine. *"You are the light of the world . . . If that light is under a bushel, it's lost something kinda crucial."** Over the years, the love light in us diminished and diminished and diminished — not because it was becoming lesser, but because we became so adjusted to living in a world without love that we forgot that love is the very life of life. We covered over that eternal flame with a false front of reaching out for things that represented love, but could never satisfy our soul in the way that only love can bless.

We are like a civilization of sleepwalkers, hypnotized into believing that there is something we have to do to be acceptable to God, when we are perfect and lovable exactly as He made us. It is as if we are a strikingly gorgeous young woman entering a beauty contest. We have been endowed with the most perfect, smooth, classically graceful features, and we are a cinch to win, far and above the competition.

---

*From "Light of the World," *Godspell* (based on the gospel according to St. Matthew) by Stephen Schwartz.

But we don't believe we are good enough to win, so we go out and invest in all kinds of make-up, which we cake on our face to the point where we do an injustice to the pure beauty that lies beneath. Then, when we come in second-place (after someone whose faith in her own beauty told her that she did not need a lavish make-up job), we think, "I knew I wasn't so beautiful!"

But we are. We are so beautiful that every star in the heavens must bow down to the Light that God has imbued in our souls. As I thrilled to hear Rev. Fuller declare over and over, "If I could only stir up God's people to remember who they are!" God loves us so much that our fears of rejection are absolutely comic. Some of us spend lifetimes wondering whether or not we really exist, while the simple solution is that there must be someone here to ask the question! We couldn't be rejected if we tried, for God would never consider rejecting Himself. The truth is that God has never rejected anyone — it is *we* who have rejected ourselves.

Because we haven't believed in ourselves as much as our Divine Mother believes in us, we invented games, manipulations, and half-communications to try to get the love that we so badly wanted to ask for, but feared rejection too much to confront. We made believe we could be outside of God's Love, and then we constructed a world based on trying to regain what we never lost. We made the only mistake we could ever make — we settled for less than who we are. We settled for less than God.

But our Heavenly Father/Mother God would not rest content with anything less than the Kingdom for us. If we attempt to suppress or quash our need to experience love, it will eventually build up within us like steam in a pressure cooker, and sooner or later it must be expressed, usually in disguised and distorted forms. These are the little tests we create, like waiting to see if someone will telephone us, when we could easily call them, or calling someone up and saying, "Guess who?" These acts are unimportant in themselves but ultimately significant because we have equated them with love. Consider the wife who asks her husband, "Would you please take the garbage out for me, dear?" which translates into, "We have been married ten years now, and I'm not sure if you still love me, so I will ask you to take out the garbage, and if you say 'Yes,' it means you do." Then when husband answers, "Can it wait just until I finish this article I'm reading?" wife screams, "You never do anything I ask you anymore!" which translates into, "I am very afraid that you don't love me anymore!" and she stomps upstairs sobbing, leaving hubby bewildered, wondering if wife still really loves him, while meanwhile both love each other immensely.

The way to outshine these hidden agendas and nourish the truth of love as the reality of life is to simply assume and remember that *when anyone asks for anything, they are asking for love,* and then give them love, no matter what the outer request. Often it does not matter whether we say "Yes" or "No," but *how we offer the gift of our response.* We can say "No" in a way that demonstrates complete caring and understanding for our brother or sister, and in so doing we are actually giving an all-important "Yes" to the person's soul, which finds its fulfillment in receiving genuine love from another human being. In fact, a kind "No" is a much greater service than a resentful "Yes," for we are *spiritual* beings and it is the *spirit* of the communication to which we respond.

If hubby would just give his wife a reassuring caress on the shoulder as he asks for a few more minutes to finish his article, he could cut through a minefield of garbled communication and answer the question that she is really asking. Or he might just punctuate his answer with "Honey," an expression of endearment that we may be tempted to write off as corny — but it sure does make us feel good to hear it. (Maybe we need to be more corny; maybe we need to try expressing the *good* feelings that we have, on the hunch that a kind "You're nice!" could make all the difference to someone out there who is having a hard day.) Or if hubby is really gutsy, he might just look his wife straight in the eye and say, "I love you very much." Or he could just take out the garbage when she asks him. It does not matter so much what he does; what matters is: is he communicating "I love you" in his answer? If he does, chances are she might just forget about the garbage and be delighted with her husband coming out of the closet as a genuine lover.

We are all genuine lovers. Some of us have come out of the closet and some of us have not, but eventually we will all know ourselves to be loving beings. This is the great awakening that is happening in so many hearts now. God will not rest — and neither will we — until we come to enjoy each other fully, as we were created to do. Our problem is not that we are unloved, but that we have not been aware that we are loved. All of our lessons on earth are designed to show us that we could never be any place other than in love.

The truth of love has led me to some premises of successful human relationships which I have found, time and time again, to be extremely powerful guides for living, and I would like to share them with you now:

1. Love is the only experience that can satisfy a human being.
2. Whenever anyone asks for anything, they are asking for love.
3. The most direct way to serve anyone is to give them love, no matter what they are asking for.
4. Pain, alienation, and conflict can seem to exist only where the awareness of the presence of love is not recognized.
5. The most powerful way to heal ourselves, one another, and our planet is to realize that love is always present, no matter what the outer circumstances suggest.
6. Every one of us has the ability to heal anything through the awareness of the presence of love.
7. Everyone and everything can be healed — indeed is already healed — because love is the power of God.

There is an affirmation that concentrates these truths into one great idea, a noble awareness which has the ability to restore any seeming loss of love between two human beings. It is an affirmation I use when I begin to feel separate from someone and I want to remind myself who we both are. If I begin to believe the lie that there is any lack of love between myself and another, I immediately affirm:

THE GOD IN ME LOVES THE GOD IN YOU;
THE GOD IN YOU LOVES THE GOD IN ME.

This affirmation is enormously powerful because it is a statement of the Truth. It is not something that we want to make happen; it is something that already is, and we want to know it. It is a statement of the fact that no matter what seems to be a problem between two people, it can be immediately and eternally healed by knowing the truth that God lives, breathes, and has His joy in every one of His human Children, and that God is eternally, ecstatically, and irrevocably in love (in fact, God *is* Love). Further, this is a declaration that love is more real than hurt and that our unity is inviolable and invulnerable. It is the light that shines away the darkness. It is the truth that gives us the courage to love.

147

We do not need to be afraid to love. For too long have we fled from the very light that can help us and heal us. For too many years, perhaps lives, have we turned our back on the lifespring of our existence. In too many relationships have we shrunk away from intimacy in fear of exposing our sensitivity, when tenderness was the redeeming Grace that sought to teach us that the hurt we feared could never harm us. For too long have we yearned for love and denied ourselves the blessings that love so deeply sought to bestow.

We are like the man who "ran and ran from my pursuer in the night. I veiled myself in the marketplace and feverishly crawled through darkened alleyways. I fell to my knees and arose and ran and fell again. I struggled under fences and held my breath as I pinned my aching body against the stone buildings to avoid detection. Finally I came to the city wall, and finding not a further heartbeat of strength to continue my flight, I fell to the ground in surrender. As the feet of my adversary drew nigh I tearfully lifted my head to see the face that I feared. It was then that I discovered my pursuer to be none other than my beloved."

For a long time I ran from love. I tried a thousand different ways to bring love into my life, when all I needed was to recognize its holy presence. I came to the momentous point at which I was in a relationship with another human being, one in which I questioned the purity of my love. I felt so attached, so unspiritual, so vulnerable. I judged myself, "Surely this cannot be God's love." I reasoned, "God's love is so much more holy than man's; dare I call this feeling 'love'? Am I a blasphemer?"

I thought and pondered, struggled and wrestled with the question of the purity of my love, begging to know if my love was real. Was God the only one capable of loving purely, or is He actually willing to share His love with Man? The real question I was asking was perhaps the most important, perhaps the only question a man asks: "Can I love?"

And because the compassion of our Father/Mother God is so great, I received an answer, one which I believe was given for all. One evening I was sitting in a group meditation, allowing Hilda to guide me into the quietness of my soul. As if by Grace, I was lifted into an illuminated view of life. Clearer and clearer grew my perception of who I am and what I have come on earth to do. Then I saw a light that shined purpose onto all persons and all lives, and it became so perfectly obvious that the heart of man *is* the heart of God. At that moment Hilda uttered these words, a blessing given for you and me, who are One:

"Children of Light, Children of Truth, Children of God:

No longer need you mark distinctions between degrees of love. No longer need you create ideas of high and low in a universe that is eternally and unalterably one. No longer need you seek the love that is your own self, for love's only purpose is to know itself.

Come, Children, rise with me, rise in love, rise into the Love that you are and have been since your birth aeons ago at the beginning of time, when God breathed forth a ray of His own soul, imbued with infinite love, and said, 'This is my child — and my child is good.' That, my Children, is who you are.

The time has come for you to know your destiny. Your destiny is not to endlessly wander in the mire of darkness; your destiny is to claim your heritage of Light that has awaited you since the blessed day your foot first touched this hallowed ground. No, Children, you cannot fall in love, for where could you fall but into the arms of your Heavenly Father/Mother God? Nor could you ever forfeit your innocence, for who could taint God? The purity of your soul is established forever in the heart of the One who made you, and your right to live in love, in peace, in joy, in happiness, is given to you now freely, fully, with the complete and whole blessing of the One who created all that is good. Thus does the loving God rejoice to the end of time in your acceptance of the reality of the Love that finds its expression through you. All blessings be upon you."

ABOUT THE AUTHOR

Alan Cohen is the author of ten popular inspirational books, including the classics, *The Dragon Doesn't Live Here Anymore* and *I Had It All the Time*. *The Celestine Prophecy* author James Redfield calls Alan "the most eloquent spokesman of the heart." Alan's column *"From the Heart"* appears in many New Thought newspapers and magazines internationally, and he is a contributing writer for the bestselling *Chicken Soup for the Soul* series.

Mr. Cohen resides in Maui, Hawaii, where he conducts seminars on spiritual awakening and visionary living. *The Mastery Training* is a highly focused small group intensive for individuals seeking to bring greater authenticity, love, and integrity to their chosen goals. *Celebrating Paradise* invites participants to reclaim their inner riches in a spirit of greater joy and aliveness. Alan also keynotes and presents workshops at many conferences and expos throughout the United States and abroad.

For a free catalog of Alan Cohen's books and audiocassettes, more information on his Hawaii seminars, and a listing of his upcoming seminars in your area, call (800) 462-3013, or write to Alan in c/o the Publicity Director at Hay House, Inc., P.O. Box 5100, Carlsbad, CA 92018-5100.

To write to Alan Cohen directly or receive more detailed information about his programs, write to The Mastery Foundation, 430 Kukuna Road, Haiku, Hawaii 96708, or call (808) 572-0001.

We hope you enjoyed this Hay House book.
If you would like to receive a free catalog featuring
additional Hay House books and products, or if you
would like information about the Hay Foundation,
please write or call:

Hay House, Inc.
P.O. Box 5100
Carlsbad, CA 92018-5100

(800) 654-5126